Alain Resnais

Susan Schenker

James Monaco is the author of *The New Wave, How to Read a Film, Media Culture, Celebrity,* and *American Film Now.* His journalism, criticism, and fiction have appeared in *The New York Times, The Village Voice, American Film, Sight and Sound,* and many other publications. He has served as a contributing editor of *MORE* and *Cineaste,* and is Associate Editor of *Take One.* In addition, he is a member of the faculty at The New School for Social Research, and has taught at Columbia University, the City University of New York, and New York University.

Alain Resnais

James Monaco

New York
Oxford University Press
1979

Copyright © 1978 by James Monaco

First published in the U.S.A. by Oxford University Press, 1979

Library of Congress Catalogue Card Number: 78-71310

Printed in the United States of America

For James Raimes and John Wright
a book which is in part
about the art of editing

Contents

Preface

Alain Resnais is partly a book about the history of the career of a rather unusual filmmaker, and partly an essay in imagination. I've tried to convey a sense of the unique moods Resnais creates for his films, as well as to challenge a number of yellowing critical axioms which have become established over the years that I consider prejudicial and biased. There is no way that any book about a film artist can give a perfect image of his oeuvre. Critics often seem to depend on the fiction that their idiosyncratic view of the subject is 'the truth, the whole truth, and nothing but the truth'.

It's not, of course, and I make no such claims for *Alain Resnais*. During the writing, which stretched over a rather long period, I was continually reminded that a critical work like this – any critical work – is far more a job of imagination than of reportage. Opinions change, not only between viewings of films, but even in the very middle of the task of writing about them. Far from being the last work on its subject, this book is only offered as a tentative guide to investigation. My working title was 'Imagining Alain Resnais'. It's more truthful, I think, than the present simple label because it makes it clear that the image of the director you are about to view is not Resnais the man and artist, not even Resnais's image of himself, but rather – very precisely – James Monaco's Alain Resnais.

Forewarned is forearmed. I hope my A.R. is entertaining and informative – certainly the real A.R. is that. But just as Resnais the filmmaker leaves a capacious and inviting space within his films for the participation of their viewers, so *Resnais* the book is designed as only half a conversation. The form fits the subject. I hope you'll join in. What follows is the truth, I believe, but definitely not the whole truth and, in fact, not precisely nothing but the truth.

I'm very grateful indeed to Alain Resnais for his gracious help in this perhaps dangerous enterprise. As a public figure he had no choice but to submit to this critical autopsy (he's been the subject of several others in the past), but nowhere is it written that he had to collaborate. He did, and I think the factual information that follows is more precise for his help.

A number of other people offered necessary assistance. Richard Seaver, Stan Lee, and David Mercer found time to talk with me about their own collaborations with Resnais. Susan Black (McGraw-Hill Films), Martin Bresnick (Audio Brandon Films), José Lopez (New Yorker Films), and Donald Rugoff and Callie Angel (Cinema 5) provided prints from which many of the stills were taken. Those companies distribute the following Resnais films in the U.S.: McGraw-Hill: *Muriel*; Audio Brandon: *Hiroshima mon amour*, *L'Année dernière à Marienbad*, *La Guerre est finie*; New Yorker: *Je t'aime, Je t'aime, Loin de Vietnam*; Cinema 5: *Stavisky...*, *Providence*.

Most of the photographs in the book are frame enlargements. A number however, come from other sources. L'Avant-Scène first published the illustrations on pp. 173 and 174; Editions de Chêne, publishers of Resnais's book *Repérages*, kindly provided most of the photographs from that book reproduced in Chapter 8. Marion Billings, Penelope Houston of *Sight and Sound*, and Catherine Verret and Variety Moszinski of the French Film Office in New York also provided stills.

Some paragraphs in Chapter 10 first appeared as a review of *Providence* in *Take One* magazine. Publisher Peter Lebensold has granted permission to reprint them. Sharon Boonshoft helped with the compilation of the bibliography. My wife, Susan Schenker, aided in numerous ways, as always.

To all: sincere thanks.

I'm especially grateful to Camille Hercot, who queried Resnais on particular details and handled research in Paris, and to Maureen Lambray, who graciously supplied photographic material for the U.S. cover. Lambray is the author of *American Film Directors* and the forthcoming *European Film Directors*. Her photographic portrait of Resnais provides a necessary complement to my own image in print.

At Secker & Warburg, Laura Morris provided necessary encouragement, and cared for the manuscript with efficiency, wit, and good sense.

James Monaco
New York City
June 1978

Alain Resnais

1. 'The Image Made in Seeing'

Alain Resnais is a modest, judicious, vaguely shy, quietly charming, diffident yet concerned man who impresses one, in person, not so much for the irony and expansiveness of his wit (although they're there, ever lurking just beneath the surface of a conversation) as with the care and conscientiousness of his intelligence. Tall, gentle, his grey hair combed carefully straight back like an overgrown, démodé crew-cut, Resnais tends to favour the same knit red shirt, grey jacket, and well-worn trenchcoat from day to day, year to year. His acquaintances aren't quite sure whether he owns one costume, carefully laundered nightly, or several, each like the other. The effect is a sense of reserve and balance. Not unaware of his public image, Resnais has posed for more than his share of publicity stills, trenchcoated on the set, viewfinder in hand, yet there is a distinct lack of braggadoccio: the persona he projects is entirely free from the verve and bravura of, say, Fellini in his broad-brimmed black fedora and expensive overcoat cape, or Godard armoured in steel-rimmed dark glasses and Bert Brecht leather jacket. There's a paradox in the image of Resnais, as there is in the man and – I believe – in the films he has made that is curious. It may be the key to our attitude towards his work.

He is at once communicative and distant, public and private. He is known for his democratic politeness. He will stop to talk with concern and attention to just about anyone who grabs him on the street, about food or comics, the weather or music, architecture or films (although given the choice he would prefer not to discuss his own). Yet one has the sense that conversation is painful for him, if only because it takes considerable energy when it is done right. Likewise, he works at his craft with equal intensity and commitment. His attention to detail is legendary, and he is at least as concerned with the precision of the final product, viewing release prints one by one to check for accuracy of colour and processing, as the more notoriously obsessive Stanley Kubrick. Yet despite – or because of – this consuming involvement with filmmaking, Resnais has completed relatively few films since his career in feature films began in 1959: seven, spread out over a nineteen-year period. None of these films has been widely popular (although *Stavisky*..., which stars Belmondo and Boyer, did quite well at the box office). And the reason may be that few people really *like* Alain Resnais's movies. They may admire them; they appreciate the talent and intelligence involved; but like the man, the films are modest and diffident – reserved and not a little distant. Resnais's work is studied for its technique or theory; his reputation as a filmmaker who must be critically confronted is assured; his name is securely inscribed in the pantheon of the modern masters of the art of filmmaking. Yet his films seldom inspire true passion, even among his proponents. Their charm is subtle, so subtle that few reviewers care to mention it. And when they are humorous, as they are surprisingly often, the humour is so cerebrally attenuated that it is often mistaken as straight.

The one quality of Resnais's films that does come through sharply and clearly in every film is what critics have taken to calling their 'intellectuality'. This is the one truism about Resnais's work that is most widespread. In a way, it has been damaging. It has marked him a 'filmmaker's filmmaker', too cerebral for the general run of popular audiences. It suggests that his films are more work than fun. And it has no doubt been responsible for producers shying away from potential projects as well as for the somewhat cool reception Resnais's films have generally been accorded at the box office.

Yet arguably Alain Resnais is no more intellectually complicated than dozens of other, mainly European, filmmakers who have in the past fifteen or twenty years been able to maintain production of a cinema that is at least as personal and thoughtful as it is entertaining and popular. If we could calculate such things, would the intellectual quotient of a representative Resnais film be measureably higher than, say, that of a typical Bergman, Antonioni, or Kubrick? I think not. And Resnais, judged mathematically in terms of the amount and intensity of intellectual subject matter in his movies, would rank considerably below such directors as Godard and Rossellini.

No, the problem isn't simply Resnais's admitted intellectuality, but rather the quality of emotion – or lack of it – for which that word is a widely understood code. What we distrust about Resnais's films is their 'emotional coldness'. Calling them 'intellectual' is simply a quick way of communicating that feeling. Critically, this is begging the question, I think. Moreover, it seems to me that this generally accepted reservation about Resnais's work is at least half the result of a remarkably prevalent misreading of his work. Perhaps the problem owes much to *L'Année dernière à Marienbad*, the film which in 1962 solidly established Resnais's reputation as an intellectual. In both that film and its predecessor, *Hiroshima mon amour*, Resnais was still a little uneasy about the tone that was eventually to characterize his work. Both the essentially subtle charm and the equally central sense of humour are erratic in those films. But beginning with *Muriel* in 1963 he finds the right track and these twin qualities begin to give more and more colour and life to Resnais's movies until, in *Stavisky...* and *Providence* in the seventies an observer has to work consciously against the films in order to avoid the effervescent charm of the former and the ebullient humour of the latter. Never has a filmmaker been so seriously hobbled by the early, quick, and superficial characterization of his style.

Clearly, this is mainly a question of audience perception. English-speaking audiences are already at a disadvantage, since so much of our sense of the attitude of a film comes from its dialogue, its literal 'tone of voice'. Irony is most easily communicated in person. Yet French-speaking observers are by no means protected from this misreading of Resnais. His irony is admittedly subtle. In an important sense, then, those who scold Resnais for his overt intelligence are correct. The emotional freight of his movies depends to an unusual extent on a complex equation of performance, the factors of which include filmmaker, product, and audience. To watch a Resnais film with different audiences is to discover how easily the humour and wit of the film can be contradicted in the performance.

This dependence on the cooperation of the observer is not surprising in a filmmaker who is so concerned with theatricality. Resnais thinks of himself as incapable of straightforward documentary realism; he is even uncomfortable with the standard mode of fictional realism which dominates contemporary cinema; and he has shown himself to be most effective when working with actors who are stage-trained to comment upon rather than mimic character, working in conjunction with audiences who provide feedback. There is a difficult critical balance here. No one contends Resnais's films are simple. But the mode in which he operates is not essentially foreign to most filmgoers. The humour and irony, at times remarkably exhilarating, are available for the taking if we simply let them reveal themselves.

Stavisky... and *Providence*, as different as they are, each prove this point. Perhaps the most important reason for *Stavisky...*'s relative commercial success was the presence on screen of Jean-Paul Belmondo and Charles Boyer. They are film stars rather than actors and their presence signalled audiences that it was O.K. to enjoy *Stavisky...* rather than necessarily to think about it. The script itself is measurably more complicated – and deals with more sophisticated ideas – than Jorge Semprun's previous film for Resnais, *La Guerre est finie*. Yet *Stavisky...* was widely accepted. Resnais's problem, and ours, is that we do often insist on taking him too seriously.

Providence is crucial proof of this dilemma. Taken straight, without humour, the film must indeed be seen as excruciatingly precious. I have seen the film with audiences that approach it that way. That's the bad news. The good news for Resnais is that enough time has passed since his reputation as a serious and difficult cinematic intellectual was established in the early sixties so that an increasingly large audience takes the film on its own terms and appreciates its distanced humour. If a generalization can be ventured, it appears that the younger the audience for *Providence* – at least in the U.S. – the better the film is received. A paradoxical position for Resnais at the age of fifty-five.

While audiences are increasingly learning to appreciate this new, and I believe more truthful, image of Alain Resnais, critics continue to elaborate upon the established, distorted persona. At best, they offer a system of coping with an elaborate web of time and memory (the graduate students' key to Resnais). At worst, they condemn the films out of hand as febrile exercises.

Pauline Kael, the doyenne of American reviewers, has expressed this view of Resnais with her usual succinct, sharp perception. In a review of *Providence* she summarized the anti-Resnais position this way:

When you go to an Alain Resnais film, you take it for granted that the only instinct that will come into play is his film instinct – his grasp of technique. Alone among major-name directors, Resnais has little grasp of character or subject; he's an innovator who hasn't got a use for his innovations. Most of the giants of film haven't been able to find the form for everything they've got in their heads; Resnais seems to have nothing but form in his. . . . What he doesn't seem to be able to do is to imbue his situations with enough feeling for these tricks to mean something to us – they're just beautiful diddles. And when form takes over and becomes an obsession, it is not just that everything else is absent – everything else is being denied.

Resnais's movies come out of an intolerable mixture of technique and culture.[1]

Now, Kael is well-known for her nearly perfect lack of sympathy with contemporary European styles in filmmaking. She's the great populist of American criticism. Yet even though this argument is dangerously overstated, it's revealing. At her best, Kael is fascinating to read because you can watch her working through with great gusto to a position. She is not unaware of the ironic wash that pervades *Providence*, nor does she ignore Resnais's previous reputation for relevance, yet she is capable of declaring that 'Resnais has little grasp of character or subject. . . . ' The major premise of the position comes a little later on. What really bothers Kael (and many others) is the ostensible lack of feeling.

It's a perfectly understandable reaction – understandable when you take into account the obtuse angle from which Kael views Resnais. A very perceptive critic of films which fall within her limited purview, Kael has never been especially interested in thinking about film as tentative and con-

1–1. Mixing technique and culture on the set of *Providence* with John Gielgud

versational. A film either works or it doesn't for Kael in a very traditional and practical Anglo-Saxon way. The tale is of primary interest ('subject or character'), the teller is of secondary interest ('he's an innovator who hasn't got a use for his innovations'), but the formula is strictly binary. The relationship between the teller and the tale (and certainly between the tale and the listener) is never taken into account.

The trouble is that it has been this relationship and its complexities which have been at the heart of French narrative art for more than fifty years. On native grounds, Resnais is not at all prized as an 'innovator'. Quite the contrary, he is well within the traditions of modernism which dictate that form is not only an acceptable subject, but a required subject. Without attention to form, the work of art operates in bad faith and whatever else it may say about character or theme is not to be trusted.

Ironically, Kael has recently taken up the cause of the New Hollywood directors – Martin Scorsese, Brian De Palma, and the like – whose own movies are just as redolent of technique as anything done in Europe in the last fifteen years but who, at least to this observer, are much more vulnerable to the charge of having nothing to say, 'nothing but form in their heads'. Kael concludes that 'Resnais's movies come out of an intolerable mixture of technique and culture'. But so do all films. We already know that she has nothing particularly against technique. What really is insupportable is the culture. Let's examine it.

Alain Resnais is one of the leading exponents of the movement in film which began in the late fifties (and is still producing much of the most interesting cinema of the seventies) known as the 'New Wave'. As an historical phenomenon, the New Wave was amorphous. Louis Malle and Roger Vadim were in the commercial cutting edge of the movement in the middle and late 1950s; Jean-Pierre Melville had been mimicking the American genres which were important models for most of the New Wave long before Godard made *A bout de souffle* in 1959, as were, in varying degrees, Jacques Demy, Georges Franju, Jacques Becker – all associated with the New Wave – and even René Clément, who was not. In the outer circle, Robert Bresson had been making films since the end of World War Two, as had the sublime comedian Jacques Tati, although these directors evinced such unique and personal talents that they clearly stand apart from the movement of the concurrent New Wave. Jean Rouch, by 1959, had begun his series of anthropological studies which were to result in the birth of cinéma vérité.

The centre of the loosely knit movement, however, was that group of filmmakers which began as critics for the magazine *Cahiers du Cinéma* under the tutelage of André Bazin. Jean-Luc Godard, François Truffaut, Claude Chabrol, Eric Rohmer, and Jacques Rivette (as well as lesser-known directors such as Jacques Doniol-Valcroze) had spent most of the period of the middle fifties working out an ideology for the new cinema in the pages of *Cahiers*. With roots in the realism of Bazin, these five very diverse critic/filmmakers developed an approach to film which insisted, above all, on an understanding of the heritage of the art. If the first generation of film was composed of explorers, and the second of craftsmen who had at best veiled contempt for the theoreticians, this third generation was to be characterized by a new respect for theory, history and analysis. Central to the conception was the *politique des auteurs* expounded first by Truffaut, then taken up by his colleagues on *Cahiers*. Each film, of necessity, had a prime author, and although it was not necessarily true historically, that author should be the director.

The ideological focal point was this sense of films as personal statements. They may be made, in practice, by committees of one hundred of more technicians and actors, but Truffaut and the others had a deeply felt need of a cinema which expressed a personal point of view. In 1948, the critic and filmmaker Alexandre Astruc had called for such a cinema. In his essay 'La Caméra-Stylo' he wrote:

To come to the point, the camera is quite simply becoming a means of expression, just as all the other arts have before it, and in particular painting and the novel. . . .it is gradually becoming a language. By language, I mean a form in which and by which an artist can express his thoughts however abstract they may be, or translate his obsessions exactly as he does in a contemporary essay or novel.[2]

The New Wave eventually fulfilled that wish. I've written in more detail elsewhere about the theory (*The New Wave: Truffaut, Godard, Chabrol, Rohmer, Rivette*, Oxford University Press, 1976) but let me summarize here a few of the major points.

If Bazin had given the *Cahiers* critics their moral basis with his realist theory, Henri Langlois ceded them their practical experience at his Cinémathèque Française. The New Wave was nurtured by the traditions of film, so that when they made the shift from theory to practice in 1959 and 1960 it is no surprise to discover that their films, in addition to being about people or ideas, were also commenting on filmmaking itself. This aesthetic self-consciousness revealed itself in different ways. Chabrol stuck closely to the Hitchcockian genre of the thriller which had fascinated him as a critic. Truffaut and Godard quickly ran through parallel series of experiments with a variety of classic genres before setting out on diametrically opposed paths. Rohmer developed a sinewy literary style which led to the nearly archaic, yet still charming series of moral tales, more closely comparable with, say, Henry James's novels than to any particular strain of cinema. Rivette, who developed more slowly, was equally absorbed with the structural idiosyncrasies of the theatrical experience.

What united these disparate filmmakers, at least for the moment, was this dual vision which allowed them to parody or comment upon the language they were employing at the same time as they used it to speak of other, more human or political concerns. It was not, after all, a very unusual development. It had happened numerous times before in this history of the older arts. The novel had developed a New Wave self-consciousness by the time of Laurence Sterne; painting reached this point at least by the time of Turner. With hindsight, it's easy to say that this rather vague ideology of the New Wave was clearly to be expected. Nevertheless, it changed our attitude towards the language of film. After 1960, every film made, whether its director intended it to or not, had to be seen with this dual vision: it was at once a story and a comment on storytelling. Simply put, it is this consciousness of the language spoken that Pauline Kael bridles at: the 'intolerable mixture of technique and culture'.

Although Alain Resnais approached his own career from a practical, rather than theorectical, standpoint he felt close to the young theoreticians of *Cahiers* in the 1950s. He had had minimal social contacts with several members of the group (and once gave Truffaut an afternoon's advice on how to re-cut a short he was working on) but he never wrote criticism himself and his career developed along different, if parallel, lines. He shows the same concern for the process that the *Cahiers* filmmakers do and he developed just as sophisticated a sense of the interrelationship between the subjects of his films and their structures. Like the *Cahiers* critics he was a product of the Cinémathèque Française and he learned much from a study of the great craftsmen of second-generation Hollywood even if he never paid such direct homage to them as did Chabrol or Truffaut. Of his relationship with the *Cahiers* group, he says,

I felt close to what they were writing. Especially the way they were thinking that American directors were not barbarians. Thanks to *Cahiers du Cinéma* we learned that American directors were just human beings and that maybe Vincente Minnelli knew more about art than any French director who was so proud of his culture![3]

More important, perhaps, Resnais's films are tempered with a concern for human character and feelings which never loses sight of the vital connection between the forms of the art and its human subjects. It's here that the New Wave separates itself distinctly from more recent generations of filmmakers who are content to mimic the past while struggling with it.

Whereas the *Cahiers* critics had arrived at these attitudes through a critical process of deduction, Resnais had travelled from the opposite direction. His training was practical rather than theoretical. Almost ten years older than Godard, Truffaut, and Chabrol he had been making films since 1936 (when he was 14 years old) and when, after the war, the others began writing about films, Resnais instead registered for courses at I.D.H.E.C. (L'Institut des Hautes Etudes Cinématographiques) and then moved directly into film production first as an actor, then as cameraman and editor. By 1947, while Godard and Truffaut were still teenagers, Resnais was already directing short documentaries. By the middle fifties, when the *Cahier* critics were just beginning to formulate their theories, Resnais, together with his friend Rémo Forlani, was already embarked on projects for feature films. Yet, in the 1960s, the practical and the theoretical converged. It becomes evident that most of New Wave theory, rather than being self-willed, was a natural organic development of the art. If *Cahiers du Cinéma* had not existed French film would nevertheless have developed along pretty much the same lines.

It is sometimes suggested that Resnais, together with his friends Agnès Varda, her husband Jacques Demy, and Chris Marker form a special wing of the New Wave. Godard termed them the 'Left Bank New Wave' because he felt their avant-garde literary leanings set them apart from the more passionate cinephiles of the 'Right Bank' *Cahiers* group. Yet even this differentiation melts under scrutiny. Resnais evinces a style that is considerably less 'literary' than Rivette's or Rohmer's, for example, and in fact even passionate movielovers Godard and Truffaut betray just as great a familiarity with books as with films.

Literary, artistic, philosophical, or cinematic – in the end it is this shared passion for the cultural heritage that marks the New Wave from film generations that had come before it. Yes, there is a vital conjuncture of technique and culture, but why must it be characterized as intolerable?

Resnais's consciousness of the cinematic heritage has always been more subtly displayed than, say, Godard's or Truffaut's. His cinema is more reserved, and especially in the earlier years of the movement, notably less ebullient. He's never desired to make a 'Gene Kelly–Stanley Donen musical' as Godard did or an homage to Hitchcock in the style of Chabrol or Truffaut. Also, unlike his contemporaries, he has been more conscious of the collaborative nature of the filmmaking process. He has always worked with screenwriters and musicians who have established strong reputations of their own outside of film and each of his films, although recognizably his, certainly is identifiable too as the work of these equal partners. Moreover, Resnais's shared attention to the connection between form and content has expressed itself in a more logical and restrained way.

The catchphrase here is 'time and memory', but Resnais himself has never quite grasped the significance of the reams of criticism in this vein. He does not think his films are especially complex and when I once asked him how he reacted to all the complicated theories that people work up about his films he replied:

I don't think my films are so complicated, do you? My reaction would be that I am ... 'flabbergasted' to see that *everything* you do during the shooting is always perceived by *somebody*![4]

Much of this seeming complexity is undoubtedly due to Resnais's editing style. It is hardly revolutionary any longer, but in 1959, 1960, and 1961 it may have seemed so. More than anyone else, Resnais and Jean-Luc Godard refreshed film language in those years by contradicting many of the clichés of the Hollywood style that had coagulated during the previous twenty years. 'At that time,' Resnais notes, 'everybody was always saying, "No, the grammar of film is complete; nothing new can be invented. Maybe we can change some things about the story or about the character, but from the point of view of form, of editing, everything has already been done – nothing new can ever be done." ' Godard's and Resnais's editing of *Hiroshima mon amour* and *A bout de souffle* was no less logical than the accredited Hollywood style. If anything, it was more rational rather than less. It greatly clarified film syntax and within a few years had trickled down to the level of the less ambitious television commercial.

No one thinks of it as revolutionary now; it is the accepted style of the day; yet Resnais still carries with him the weight of the reputation for being 'experimental', in the chariest sense of that word.

There are several possible explanations for Resnais's free-style editing, which treats film time as a completely malleable material, rather than following a strict and literal narrative line. Godard had worked out complicated theories about the relationship of montage and *mise en scène*. Resnais suggests that his own affinity for the jump cut, the flashback, and what later came to be called the 'flashforward' had a much more mundane genesis.

Maybe you will think this is a joke, but I don't know if it is. It could come from the fact that when I was a kid I was fascinated by Milton Caniff's cartoon 'Terry and the Pirates,' but it was an impossible task to find that story in France because it would be published for two weeks and then disappear. Then I would find it in Italian, and then *that* would disappear too. And after that there was a war and so I had to read 'Terry and the Pirates' in complete discontinuity. Well, I discovered that it gave the story a lot of emotion to know Terry when he was fourteen, and then when he was, say, 24, after which I would make up myself what had happened to him when he was 22, or 17.[5]

This propensity for discontinuous editing reached a climax in *Je t'aime, je t'aime* (1968), an exhilarating collage of episodes and moments from a man's life which I consider his most brilliant technical achievement. Sadly, it was also his greatest box-office failure and was at least partly responsible for his six-year absence from the screen in the late sixties and early seventies. When he returned, with *Stavisky...* in 1974, it was with a much more conventional editing style.

While the received critical opinion has always been that Resnais was a theorist of time and memory, his approach to this area of film art is considerably less elaborate, just as the impetus which led him to experiment with malleable film time was more mundane. 'I've always refused the word "memory" a propos my work,' he declares. 'I'd use the word "imagination."' [6]

It's not a word often used to talk about art these days. It's reminiscent of romantic theory rather than post-modernism, of poetry rather than film, yet it is a surprisingly useful key to Resnais's cinematic world. Interestingly enough, it also connects him with a long literary tradition that stretches back past symbolist and romantic poetry to the Renaissance and earlier.

In *Leviathan* Hobbes defined imagination this way:

after the object is removed, or the eye shut, we still retain an image of the thing seen,

1–2. With Claude Rich and Olga Georges-Picot on the set of *Je t'aime, je t'aime*

though more obscure than when we see it. And this is it, the Latines call *Imagination*, from the image made in seeing... IMAGINATION therefore is nothing but *decaying sense*; and is found in men, and many other living Creatures, as well sleeping, as waking....when we would express the *decay*, and signify that the Sense is fading, old, and past, it is called *Memory*. So that *Imagination* and *Memory*, are but one thing, which for divers considerations hath divers names.

What better way to describe the felt reality of the film experience? 'The image made in seeing.' Hobbes is obviously struggling with his definition of imagination (just as many others struggled after him). That central phrase is in some respects tautological. If the image is the thing seen, what other image could there be than that made in seeing? But the experience of film has heightened our ability to understand the differentiation he intended. There is the image that exists for itself, the picture, and the image 'made in seeing', the conception, which does not imitate so much as analyses or comments upon. The image is perceived reality. Penelope Mortimer, who once worked for a short while with Resnais on one of the several unrealized projects of the early seventies, describes his struggle (and her own)

with the enormous enterprise – familiar to so many artists, and completely foreign to a few – of approaching reality through the imagination, of approaching the imagination through reality.[7]

It's hard not to sound romantic and ethereal when discussing the cinematic process in these terms, but there is a hard kernel of truth here. For Hobbes, imagination 'is nothing but *decaying sense*'. Yet film captures and freezes these phenomena. For anyone who has worked with the medium, that is the most striking quality about it. Alain Resnais's career is best explained as a quest to discover the uses of that quality. If memory is 'fading, old, and past' sense, then memory has little to do with Resnais's cinema since every cinematic image is, on the face of it, the equal of any other.

Etymologically and semantically the cluster of *imago* words reinforces this sense of discovery. Within 'image', for example, a number of meanings strive for historical supremacy. There is the original physical sense, as well as the more modern connotations of conception (or mental image) and figure or trope (as is literary theory). Underlying this collection of potential significances is a root tension between ideas of imitation (which word itself is probably related etymologically) or copying, and creation or fantasy. Imagination then is neither 'realistic' nor unrealistic, but simply the sum total of our cognitive dealings with the world around us.

Recently, 'image' has been redefined in terms of publicity and celebrity (a usage which in all probability has superseded the earlier meanings). Resnais is equally sensitive to this new, dominant connotation of the word. It is, after all, mainly the product of film language. As Raymond Williams has described it, 'The sense of image in literature and painting had already been developed to describe the basic units of composition in film. This technical sense in practice supports the commercial and manipulative processes of image as "perceived" reputation or character.'[9]

Looked at from this perspective, Resnais's 'tricks' are far more than the 'beautiful diddles' Pauline Kael perceives; they are attempts at dealing with the way we comprehend the world, and what enterprise could be more useful? At times they may seem cool and distant. At times they seem – indeed, consciously *are* – bluntly mysterious, or comically incomprehensible. But that's the way it always is with these images made in seeing. As in life, so in film.

Really, Alain Resnais's films, far from being the complicated and tortuous intellectual puzzles they are reputed to be, are rather simple, elegant, easily understood – and felt – investigations of the pervasive process of imagination. It doesn't even take much imagination to enjoy them. All that is necessary is an understanding that we are watching not stories, but the telling of stories. Far from being a forcible, new intellectual twist, this is simply a little refreshing honesty. In life, we watch stories, in film we always, perforce, must watch the telling. There is no other way, so why not admit it within the limits of the movie?

Resnais isn't unusually modern. In fact, he would be right at home in the last century when imagination – the word as well as the thing – had more immediate currency. Here, for example, is Charles Baudelaire's meditation on the phenomenon. Like Hobbes's, it's an unwitting yet richly allusive description of cinema. It is also a nice apologia for artists like Resnais who consider imagination a subject as well as a tool:

It is imagination which has taught man the moral values of colour, shape, sound, and perfumes. At the beginning of the world, imagination created analogy and metaphor. Imagination dissolves all creation. Remassing and reordering her materials by principles which come out of the depths of the human soul, imagination makes a new world, even a new realm of sensory experience. And as imagination has created this world (one may say this, I think, even in a religious sense), it is appropriate that the same faculty should govern it.[9]

2. A Réaliser

If 'imagination', the 'reordering and remassing' of reality, as Baudelaire defined it, is the abstract work of cinema, 'réalisation', the French verb for filmmaking, very well defines the concrete job. The 'new realm of sensory experience' that imagination yields must be made real – visible and audible – before the equation is complete. Alain Resnais, since childhood, has had a special need to realize, to 'make real', to 'fulfil' the images which surround us all. If imagination 'dissolves creation', realization reconstitutes it.

Born in Vannes in Brittany, 3 June 1922, Resnais suffered from asthma as a child, eventually leaving school because of his poor health. At home, in his room, he read voraciously, becoming especially fond of the literary guardian angel of all recluses, Proust. It's tempting to ascribe inordinate influence to this early master of the sensibilities of time and memory – and no doubt Resnais's films do owe much to him – yet Proust was only one of the poles which served as foci for Alain's developing personal sense of imagination. He was also addicted to comic books (and has continued his study of the art form in later life becoming Vice President of the Centre d'Etude des Littératures d'Expression Graphique and an adviser to *Giff-Wiff*, a journal devoted to comics). He learned Italian just so that he could follow some of the strips that weren't available in France and, as we've already noted, suggested not entirely without seriousness that his basic sense of film montage was formed during those early years reading comics catch-as-catch-can.

This confluence of high culture and popular culture must have been singularly important for the boy who was going to grow up to become one of the most important directors to bridge the gap between the two formerly antagonistic and mutually exclusive cultures. Had Resnais been exposed to the full course of a French secondary education he may very well have been much less able to reconcile the adventures of Albertine with the drastically contrasting exploits of Terry and the Pirates.

2–1. High culture and popular culture: fantasy cartoon (above) with pulp novels on either side, Magritte print to the right, science fiction illustrations behind Claude Rich's head

More important perhaps than these early cultural influences was the unusual gift he received from his parents when he was 12 years old: a small 8-mm camera. His father, a pharmacist, was not especially wealthy, so that such a present for a young boy was remarkable in 1934. Resnais took to learning the technique of filmmaking immediately, and spent many hours in the medieval streets of Vannes filming his friends doing improvisations. 'As soon as his films were developed,' recalls a childhood pal, 'he would invite all his friends to come see them. He had built a little movie theatre in a tiny, uncomfortable room, but he'd managed to equip it with real wooden movie theatre seats, which we took great pleasure in banging up and down.'[1]

Within months, young Alain had conceived his first feature film, 'L'Aventure de Guy', based on a scenario he found in a magazine for amateur movie makers. Apparently, the film no longer exists and none of Resnais's young friends were equally precocious movie critics, otherwise we might have some record of the event. He moved on quickly to a more ambitious project, a version of *Fantômas*, the famous silent serial. But the actors weren't quite up to Resnais's standards of melodramatic fantasy, however, and he never finished the film.

In May 1939, shortly before his 17th birthday, Alain left Vannes for Paris to act as an assistant to the Pitoëff company at the Théâtre des Mathurins. 'The curious thing,' he later said, 'was that I thought I didn't like theatre. All of a sudden it became the most important thing in the world to me, so much so that I decided to become an actor.'[2] For the next eight years, his interest vacillated between stage and screen. Between 1940 and 1942 he studied acting with René Simon, then in 1943, entered I.D.H.E.C. He left in 1945 to do his army service. He acted with a company called Les Arlequins in Constance, the French occupation zone.

In 1946, he returned to Paris and set about building a career in film in earnest. Gérard Philipe lived in the same apartment house as Resnais on the rue du Dragon and Resnais wrote a scenario for a surrealistic silent short for Philipe to act in called 'Schéma d'une identification'. Shot in 16 mm in an unheated apartment, it was his first adult effort. Resnais screened it several times for friends and invited guests at his apartment, but no one apparently now remembers it and the print is lost.

No trace exists either of Resnais's first full-length film, also shot in 1946. *Ouvert pour cause d'inventaire* was the title, and it too seems to have been surrealist. Again, it was privately screened, but those of his friends who remember it have hazy recollections at best.

By 1947, the 25-year-old filmmaker was ready to move on to more commercial work. He had apprenticed as cinematographer, assistant director and assistant editor on a couple of features and an advertising film. In 1947, he made a short with Marcel Marceau (whom he had met through Les Arlequins) entitled 'La Bague', another short, 'L'Alcöol tue', which was shot in two days in a quarry near Meaux and involved a group of workmen and a priest, and, most important, a series of studies of painters in 16 mm which led directly to his first commercial success in 35 mm, 'Van Gogh'. His 'Visites à' Lucien Coutaud, Felix Labisse, Hans Hartung, César Doméla, and Henri Goetz were important and invaluable experiments in the crucial relationship of montage and mise en scène. As Resnais himself described it:

The problem was to find out if painted trees, painted houses, and painted characters could, by way of montage, fulfil the roles of real objects and if, in this case, it was possible to substitute for the observer the interior world of an artist for the world that photography revealed.[3]

Resnais's moving camera did indeed bring these worlds alive. 'Van Gogh', which Resnais filmed along similar lines in 16 mm at the urging of Gaston Diehl impressed a young producer with Pierre Braunberger's company enough so that he convinced this important distributor to blow it up to 35 mm for release. It won a double prize in 1948 at the Venice Biennale and two years later was awarded an American Oscar. Alain Resnais's future was assured.

Resnais made two more films on art and artists for Braunberger in 1950, 'Gauguin' and 'Guernica', the latter probably the more successful of the two. By this time he had developed a solid reputation as a short-filmmaker of considerable talent. If short films were taken more seriously, it would have been clear that the New Wave, based on Astruc's theory of the caméra-stylo and evincing a new technical freedom, had already been born. As it was, Resnais's position was clear enough to committed cineastes so that Godard could later write:

If the short film hadn't existed, Alain Resnais surely would have invented it. . . .From the blind, trembling pans of 'Van Gogh' to the majestic travelling shots of 'Styrène' what in effect do we see? A survey of the possibilities of cinematographic technique, but such a demanding one, that it finishes by surpassing itself, in such a way that the modern young French cinema could not have existed without it. For Alain Resnais more than anyone else gives the impression that he completely started over at zero.[4]

High praise indeed from the filmmaker who more than anyone else wanted in the 1960s to take cinema back to zero to start over again.

In a way, Resnais was too far ahead of his time. Producers were willing to let this young French cinema exist in the fifties, but only in the commercially limited world of the short film. Resnais tried several times to put together features, but was frustrated until 1959, when Godard, Truffaut, Chabrol, Malle, and the younger proponents of the New Wave had caught up.

2–2. A sequence from *Van Gogh*: 'blind, trembling pans'

In addition to 'Van Gogh', 'Gauguin', and 'Guernica', the shorts Resnais made in the fifties strangely mirror the features he was later to shoot in the sixties. Gaston Bounoure, an old friend, and author of an informative study of Resnais's films in the Seghers 'Cinéma d'aujourd'hui' series, goes so far as to match five of the shorts with the features. 'Guernica' and *La Guerre est finie* both deal with Spain; 'Nuit et Brouillard' and *Hiroshima mon amour* with the Second World War; 'Les Statues meurent aussi' and *Muriel* both have something to do with African versus French culture; 'Toute la mémoire du monde' and *L'Année dernière à Marienbad* are both architectural memories (here the similarity is really quite remarkable); finally, 'Le Chant du Styrène' and *Je t'aime, je t'aime* are abstract structural studies.

'Les Statues meurent aussi', commissioned by Présence Africaine in 1950 and finished three years later, describes the disintegration of African art as a result of the cultural imperialism of French colonial powers. The film was banned in France for 12 years after it was made and has been little seen since. For Resnais, it was an obvious extension of his work with paintings in the films that had preceded it. 'Les Statues meurent aussi' added the political element to the cultural mix. Art is not simply evidence; it lies between a culture and the people who create that culture. In the words of Chris Marker, who wrote the commentary and co-directed with Resnais:

> We want to see their suffering, serenity, humour, even though we don't know anything about them. Colonisers of the world we want everything to talk to us: animals, the dead, statues. . . . [5]

But statues die also. We kill them with a look.

'Nuit et Brouillard' ('Night and Fog'), Resnais's best-known and most successful short, was completed in 1955. Confronted with the challenge of capturing on film the enormity of the horror of the German death camps, he realized that standard documentary techniques would be useless – even counterproductive. They could only have the effect of humanizing the incomprehensible terror, of making it comprehensible, and therefore diminishing it. He discovered – maybe fortuitously – the only artistic device that works in this situation: the leverage provided by the irony of distancing.

'Nuit et Brouillard' deals more with our memory of the camps, our mental images of them, than with the camps as they actually existed, for the memories are real and present, as are the physical remains through which his restless camera ceaselessly tracks. From frozen photographs of the actuality at the end of the war and from contemporary colour footage of the remains of the camps, Resnais composes a dialectic which extrapolates backwards towards the unimaginable horror. Jean Cayrol, who wrote the text and narrates the film, was a former inmate himself. Resnais was adamant about Cayrol's partici-

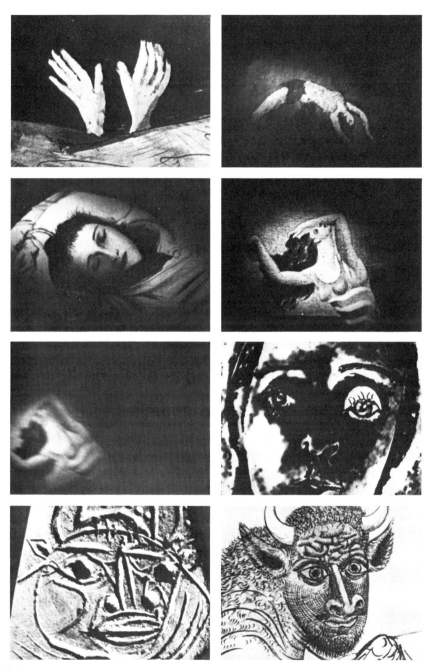

2–3. A sequence from *Guernica*

pation since he felt no one who had not experienced the camps had the moral authority to speak about them.

Cayrol's narrative is intentionally understated, almost ironic at times, and this further adds to the power of the distancing effect. It was vitally important for both Cayrol and Resnais to describe the phenomenon of the camps not as a fact of dead history, but as evidence of a present reality. It isn't the camps that count, it's the ability to build them: and that is still a very real and present talent.

Cayrol concludes his narrative with this quiet warning:

And there are those of us who look concernedly at these ruins as if the old Concentration monster were dead in the rubble, those of us who pretend to hope before this distant picture, as if the plague of the camps had been wiped out, those of us who pretend to believe that all this happened long ago, and in another country, who never think to look around us, who never hear the cry that never ends.[6]

The censors, once again, however, heard Resnais and Cayrol very clearly. 'Nuit et Brouillard' was withdrawn from the Cannes Festival of 1956. The ostensible reason was that the French government did not want to offend another participating government. Yet what really disturbed the censors was the challenge the film presented to the French to recognize their own complicity in the extraordinary crime of the death camps. They glossed over, for the most part, the inferences of the narrative to seize on one particular image, a shot of about five seconds which showed the Pithiviers assembly camp. In the control tower a French gendarme was clearly visible. This visual evidence of collaboration was intolerable to the authorities. After two months of negotiations, the producers of the film agreed to alter the image (and the evidence of history) by covering the gendarme's uniform. It would be another fifteen years before Marcel Ophuls's *Le Chagrin et la pitié* would bring the dirty secret of collaboration back into the light.

2–4–11. The Essential images of *Nuit et Brouillard*: 4. Contemporary documentary: 'A peaceful landscape'. 5. Historical documentary: 'Nacht und Nebel': a classification for detainees. 6. Historical documentary: night and fog. 7. A tracking shot of a railway, overgrown with weeds today, matches with.... 8. ... A tracking shot of the camp's latrines, empty, quiet, and peaceful now. 9. 'Picture-postcard crematoria' today. 10. 'The only sign – this ceiling scored by fingernails.' 11. A mountain of women's hair: 'The skill of the Nazis is child's play today'.

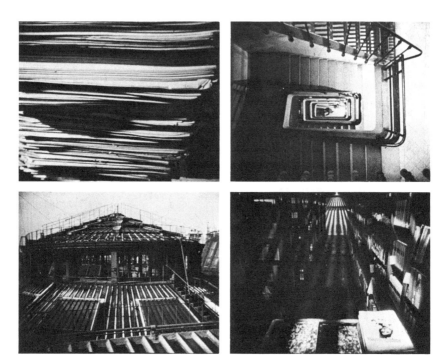

2–12–15. The textures of *Toute la mémoire du monde*: newspapers, staircases, roofs (compare with the shot from *Stavisky...* 9–18 on p. 184), endless corridors with grilled shadows.

'Toute la mémoire du monde' (1956) had no such censorship problems. It is a documentary evocation of the Bibliothèque Nationale which becomes, for Resnais, an objective correlative of our collective memory, a maze of corridors and stacks out of the fiction of Jorge Luis Borges. Like its predecessors, it is a film about material evidence rather than theoretical conjecture. Made for one of the cultural divisions of the Foreign Ministry, 'Toute la mémoire' annoyed a few people when it was released: cultural propaganda should be more didactic they thought. Resnais had instead filmed a lyrical paean to his own pleasure in one hundred kilometers of corridors full of half-forgotten knowledge. He pays tongue-in-cheek homage to Mandrake the Magician and to Harry Dickson, his favorite pulp hero, and concludes:

readers, seated in front of their own morsels of universal memory will put together end to end the fragments of a single secret, which perhaps has a very beautiful name: it's called 'happiness'.

24

Not the usual rhetoric of a government documentary.

Resnais's next project was for a feature film, the script of which was to be written by his friend Rémo Forlani, who had done the narrative for 'Toute la mémoire', 'Un Dimanche tous ensemble', about a group of adolescents wandering around Paris one Sunday was to be shot using cinéma vérité techniques (although the phrase had yet to be invented) and a lot of improvisation. According to John Ward, the film was never made because Resnais felt uncomfortable with the technique. The year following, Resnais and Forlani attempted an opposite tack. 'L'Ile noire' was to have been a highly stylized feature in which the actors would have worn masks. Again, the preparation came to nought, although Forlani later wrote a script which was filmed by another director. 1957 also saw the completion of 'Le Mystère de l'atelier 15', the only finished episode from a series of forty films which Resnais and Forlani had planned whose general title and subject was to have been 'L'Organization du travail'. 'Le Mystère' deals with industrial disease. For reasons unknown Resnais turned over the completion of the film to his assistant, André Heinrich.

2–16. 'Mandrake, King of Magic ... War in the World of X Dimensions'

2–17. The odyssey of the book ends here as a pair of hands and shadows coordinate it within the collective memory

Throughout the mid-fifties, while planning features and completing shorts, Resnais was also working as editor on other people's films, sometimes, it would appear, for the money it brought in, at other times out of a more genuine commitment. Agnès Varda's 'La Pointe courte', Jacques Doniol-Valcroze's *L'Oeil du maître*, William Klein's *Broadway By Night*, and François Reichenbach's *Paris à l'automne* are among the films he cut during this period.

Resnais's last short, 'Le Chant du Styrène', shot in 1958 is perhaps his most unusual effort, even if it is much simpler in conception and less ambitious than its predecessors. It is just what its title announces it to be: a song about plastic – an 'industrial' made for the Société Pechiney to celebrate their product. It does so with masterful abandon. The film has a text by Raymond Queneau written in alexandrines because, Resnais explained:

I was thinking of the didactic poetry of Boileau and Malherbe and it seemed to me that a text in verse would be more effective, pedagogically, and then I felt in a confused way that there was a connection between the alexandrine and cinemascope. [7]

2–18–21. The patterned webs of the Song of Styrene in reverse industrial order from end product back through the petroleum cycle (Anamorphic frames).

A materialist hymn, 'Le Chant du Styrène' traces the manufacture of polystyrene backwards from finished product, 'across the desert of pipework, towards the raw material, towards the abstract matter'. Gaston Bounoure is right to pair 'Le Chant' with *Je t'aime, je t'aime* for, as dissimilar as the two films may at first seem, both represent the pure Resnais style and are buoyant exercises of it. In both, Resnais was free to do what his critics have always censured him for doing but what he seldom does: put style before content.

'Le Chant du Styrène' is easily the most remarkable 'industrial' film ever made, both visually and narratively. The black and white reproductions here don't convey half the exhilaration Resnais finds in the particoloured purity of polystyrene. The liquid lines of the production stream provide an ingratiating form for the montage of the film against which is contrasted Queneau's drole verse. (Resnais had originally wanted it sung.) It is a mathematical word game that parallels the rhythms of the chemical process in mock heroic couplets:

O temps, suspends ton bol!* O matière plastique!
D'où viens tu? Qui es-tu? et qu'est-ce qui explique
Tes rares qualités? De quoi donc es-tu fait?
D'où donc es-tu parti? Remontons de l'objet
a ses aïeux lointains! Qu'à l'envers se déroule
Son histoire exemplaire. Voici d'abord le moule.

O time, hold your pill! O plastic material!
Whence come you? Who are you? and who can explain
Your rare qualities? Of what, in fact, are you made?
Where, in fact, do you come from? Let the objects return
to their distant forebears. As backwards the story unrolls
of their exemplary history. First: here's the mould.

Queneau runs on like this for 70 more lines of classical heroic chemistry before
drawing breathlessly to a saleable conclusion in which 'la mutation chimique'
rhymes in more ways than one with sales at 'prix unique'.

An enjoyable ending to Resnais's career as the foremost short-film director
in France since the war.

During this extended journeymanship, Resnais had developed precise work
habits – patterns which tell a good deal about the work as well as the man. Like
his contemporaries in the New Wave he worked intimately with a small group
of colleagues and friends. Unlike Godard, Truffaut and the rest of the *Cahiers*
critics, however, he did not make it a point of auteurist honour to dominate the
construction of scenarios. Although everyone who has written for Resnais
attests to his close and intense involvement with script development, ever since
'Guernica' at least Resnais has depended heavily on screenwriters with strong
literary reputations. Indeed, he has made the opposition between auteur and
author one of the main dynamics of his films.

Superficially, he explains this by noting that to write the film himself and
then shoot it would be to do the same job twice:

... to write a film myself I would need maybe three or four years [he told me]. I don't
enjoy very much directing something I have written. I don't know why, but it's no fun

---

* Lamartine's famous cri de coeur:

> O temps, suspends ton vol! et vous, heures propices,
>   Suspendez votre cours!
> Laissez-nous savourer les rapides délices
>   Des plus beaux de nos jours!

for me. It bores me a little. Or maybe it's because I am hiding from responsibility. Who knows?[8]

But since the people he chooses to write for him are established artists in their own right with strongly recognizable styles and concerns the tension between their aims and Resnais's own becomes one of the sources of interest in the films. Of the shorts, 'Guernica' was written by Paul Eluard, 'Nuit et Brouillard' by Cayrol, 'Le Chant du Styrène' by Queneau. When he turned to features, Resnais at first chose to work with novelists of the nouveau roman school (Marguerite Duras: *Hiroshima mon amour*; Alain Robbe-Grillet: *L'Année dernière à Marienbad*), then rejoined Cayrol for a feature (*Muriel*) before moving on to Jorge Semprun (*La Guerre est finie* and, later, *Stavisky...*) and Jacques Sternberg (*Je t'aime, je t'aime*). *Providence* was a slight departure in that it was written by a playwright, David Mercer, rather than a novelist. None of these people had had much experience – if any – with film before they collaborated with Resnais. Yet remarkably, four of them – Cayrol, Duras, Semprun, and Robbe-Grillet – have gone on to direct films themselves.

If they had not already established themselves as writers before turning to cinema, we could almost speak of a school of Resnais. The director explains the phenomenon this way:

I think it's because I was not choosing these screenwriters because they were writers but because they had a hidden desire to make films! So I enjoyed seeing them make films after because that was the proof for me that I was right.[9]

Proof in a way, I suppose, but none of the four has done as well on his or her own as with Resnais. Duras has been the most prolific and has, in fact, established such a strong reputation as a filmmaker in the seventies that it has almost eclipsed her fame as a novelist. For this observer at least, however, her structuralist experiments are a little too precious for Duras to be taken seriously as an important filmmaker. Robbe-Grillet, too, seems to have been spending more time behind a camera during the last ten years than behind a pen. He has developed a very precise style (as has Duras) but it seems to be entirely devoted to sado-masochist fantasies – often antifeminist – in the guise of materialist mysteries. Cayrol and Semprun have directed too few films to support a judgement.

Writing a film for Resnais is not an easy matter. The process often extends over a period of years. Jacques Sternberg, for example, first met Resnais in 1962; it was five years before *Je t'aime, je t'aime* was shot. During this period there are constant exchanges between director and author. All of Resnais's screenwriters make it clear that he never imposes his views on them. All of them are equally insistent that the finished product – somehow – strongly bears his mark. When the script has reached its final stage it represents a quiet collaboration between writer and director and, as a result, Resnais changes very little of the scenario during the shooting. Resnais likes to have his films mapped out precisely before he begins so that he can pay attention to realizing the script in the mise en scène.

Conversations with Resnais are liberally punctuated with the word 'process'. It is a hallmark for him, and it is clear that he considers his movies to be products of that process rather than willed art objects. Often, it seems, he is almost a bystander as the film grows by itself, according to its own rules of process.

This process is not so much logical as biological; organic rather than intellectual. In the first place, it is the sum of the intricate network of collaborations among director, writer, cinematographer, actors, designers, musicians, and other technical personnel. More important, perhaps, is the Pirandellian dialectic between characters and actors, actors and director, director and audience. Resnais speaks often of the surprising resilience of imagined characters. They do take on a life of their own in a way that only writers and filmmakers truly understand.

Thus 'biological dialectic' (it is Resnais's phrase) evinces itself in every area of production. The eternal, twin themes of time and memory, for example, which stand out so strongly for most viewers in his films, are always handled dialectically. It is not the poetry of memory nor its characteristic dream quality that attracts Resnais (although those are two elements that have considerable cinematic value), but rather the astonishing contrast between our experience of the past and our memory of it. We have perhaps been more painfully conscious of the phenomenon of memory, even in a political sense, during the past fifteen years. Santayana's dictum – 'Those who do not remember the past are condemned to repeat it' – seems to have become the byword of the seventies, a period which even in popular culture does not seem to have a distinct style of its own and which has been borrowing voraciously from previous twentieth-century decades. In this respect, Resnais's obsession with remembrance and repetition is unusually timely.

Dialectically, the clash between the memory and the experience yields a third thing, possibly closer to organic biological reality than either. This is the job of the imagination. The job of realization is infinitely harder. Resnais has often been quoted as complaining that making a truly timely film is impossible. By the time shooting begins, months have passed, contemporary jargon has changed – slightly but significantly. By the time the film is edited, processed and released it is therefore hopelessly out of date: a relic of a moment past that attempts to capture a pluperfect moment which is always receding beyond reach. It's a fine point, perhaps, but a real problem for Resnais.

The oppositions of experience and memory are even mirrored in the structures of the films. Resnais often insists on a groundbase of a contrasting subplot to set off the main theme of the film: the Trotsky subplot in *Stavisky...*, for example, or the science-fiction framework of *Je t'aime, je' t'aime*. His fascination with the flashback (and the 'flashforward') is also exemplary: it gives him the opportunity to describe the contemporary psychological reality of the character in all its dimensions, since – as this boyhood devourer of Proust must well know – the premonition, the aftertaste, and the imagined reality are often better indexes than present fact.

Practically, rather than theoretically, this approach to filmmaking was inevitable for Resnais. His own experience with the medium as cameraman and editor showed him in practice the formidable power of film to analyse the phenomenon of time. As a scientific tool, the film medium has found some of its most useful applications in revealing the nature of phenomena that happen either too quickly or too slowly for the human brain to comprehend them. Film performs the same functions for time that the inventions of the microscope and telescope do for space.

On a more human level, the elemental ability of the editor to put one image beside another, to repeat, to reverse, and to break down the flow of time has significant consequences. This is the real magic of montage. Film tells the truth, even when it doesn't. Hitchcock proved this point to his chagrin with his experiment in *Stage Fright*: he discovered that audiences simply would not accept a flashback that 'lied'. Lies can be told, but they cannot be seen. Any piece of film has, inherently, just as great a realistic value as any other. Therefore, if images distort each other, as they often do in Resnais's films, spectators must shift the level of their trust. The pictures of 'reality' become just as problematic as the pictures of 'fantasy'. Nothing is fact; everything is imagined. Epistemologically, that is a valuable lesson to learn since we never observe our surroundings without filtering them through a complex idiosyncratic set of conflicting emotions, personal references, and half-felt memories. Machines give valid readings; people never do. Luckily.

It is no surprise to learn that one of Resnais's favourite perpetual projects for the last several years has been a film, half documentary, half fiction, that would deal with the biochemical theories of Henri Laborit on the workings of the human brain. Basically, his work has been driven by an abiding fascination with the phenomena of perception and, like the great Roberto Rossellini, Resnais's later years may just be devoted to exploring the past – or more precisely, our perceptions and uses of it – more as science than as fiction. 'Toute la mémoire du monde', 'Le Chant du Styrène', and the other shorts of the fifties all point in this direction.

Meanwhile, the characters of Resnais's films lead lives of their own. This too is a sign of the biology of the dialectic. He is often accused of producing programmatic narratives in which style and theme dominate character, but from his own point of view quite the reverse is true. He has often felt a slight antagonism towards characters who won't allow him and his screenwriters to say precisely what they want to say. The complicated narrative structure of his films is not imposed on them, it grows naturally and organically from the characters themselves:

My idea [he explains] is that the complexity of the structure of the film comes – *must* come – from the characters of the story. If, in *Muriel*, the characters are *very* complex, everybody is thinking a lot, and so it leads to a very complicated structure. But in *La Guerre est finie*, Diego is a kind of – not too simple – but not very subtle character. He has two or three motivations, but he is not a mysterious character at all....so it would have been silly to impose a kind of complicated structure with *La Guerre est finie*.[10]

The much remarked upon 'flashforwards' of *La Guerre est finie* grew for Resnais out of the character of Diego. As a political operative for more than 25 years Diego, it seemed to Semprun and Resnais, would quite naturally often think of the consequences of his actions, and have premonitions of them.

In speaking of them, Resnais often suggests that once the characters have been 'invented' they take hold of a film and push it in directions it wouldn't otherwise have gone. While he is regarded by some as more politically oriented than most of the New Wave (on the strength, one supposes, of the subject matter of several of the films) he has often been criticized for the political direction his films take. 'If you have some respect for the character,' he explains,

the character very often takes over. In *Hiroshima mon amour*, for example, there were three or four lines that were more clear politically, and which Marguerite Duras and myself enjoyed. But when they were spoken by the actor it did not fit with the character; it became silly because we had the feeling that it was like a commentary and it did not work. We discovered that a character becomes a real character when he begins to do things we don't approve.[11]

The same thing has happened with most of his films. He does not approve of the characters in *Muriel*, but 'Jean Cayrol and I could not make them act differently'. With *Stavisky...* he and Semprun had originally wanted to make a more documentary kind of film which would have treated the financial and political dimensions of Stavisky's story more fully, but they discovered that, 'little by little, the character was "invading" the picture....The character took over, but it was not at all on purpose. It was a kind of biological process'.

Something is going on there, and Alain Resnais wants to find out what it is. He once characterized his films as attempts, 'still very crude and primitive, to approach the complexity of thought, its mechanism.' Imagination, the first, creative stage of this mechanism, is a relatively simple matter as compared with 'réalisation', the second, analytical stage. Together, the two form the biological dialectic which has absorbed most of Alain Resnais's energies for thirty years.

3. False Documentary

Early in 1958, Resnais received a commission to do a short documentary on the atomic bomb. He worked on it for a month or two with little success. He was blocked. There seemed to be no way to do the film on the bomb without remaking 'Nuit et Brouillard'. The facts of the bomb were different enough from the facts of the death camps, it is true, but the perceptual effect was the same: memories, knowledge of incomprehensible suffering, pain, and death. Since it was the perception of it rather than the event that interested Resnais, the two films added up to the same thing.

He went to the producer to tell him that he couldn't do the film, then, as a joke, added, 'Of course if someone like Marguerite Duras were interested....'[1] She was. *Hiroshima mon amour* was the result: a documentary cum love story that won a double prize at Cannes in 1959 (just beating *Les Quatre Cents Coups*) becoming an immediate international classic and the opening clarion of the New Wave.

The film's genesis was rooted in an agreement for a Japanese-French co-production which had the following requirements attached to it: one major character must be French, the other Japanese, and at least one major sequence must be shot in each country with the technicians of that country. It was the kind of professional puzzle that Resnais had cut his teeth on in industrials and documentary shorts. *Hiroshima mon amour* is a critical puzzle, as well. It remains by far Resnais's most complicated, difficult, confusing, and treacherous essay in the social, political, and linguistic/semiological ramifications of film. This is partly intentional, but by no means entirely so.

Let's begin by making it clear that there are two distinct films here. The film the cinephile sees, with the benefit of theory, is most certainly a complex knot of cinematic problematics – enough goes on (or does not go on) in *Hiroshima* to keep an advanced film class busy for a year. But the film the public saw at Cannes and, shortly, around the world – the film that was a popular success and helped insure the stability of Resnais's career in the

3–1. Resnais on the set of *Hiroshima mon amour* with Emmanuelle Riva and Eiji Okada, the opposite poles of the co-production

early sixties – is not at all complex. Narratively, it is, in fact, considerably simpler than the kinds of stories audiences were used to in the 1950s. It is limited, essentially, to two characters; it is a classic, almost clichéd love story of the sort that could have been easily understood fifty years ago; and while its montage is mildly adventurous (Resnais cuts according to his own sense of narrative, which was certainly not Hollywood's but was nevertheless clear and logical), it is also pointed, direct, and effective. No perceptual mysteries here.

If the immediately perceived film is not especially difficult to comprehend, then what are the critical problems that have resulted in so many analytical essays being written about the film since 1959? They revolve, I think, around two related questions having to do with problems of cinematic discourse:

1. It is impossible to do a film about the bomb. Resnais was unable to complete a short documentary, but nevertheless had little trouble finishing a longer film that not only included documentary footage, but also told a fictional story – two fictional stories, in fact. Marguerite Duras called this approach 'false documentary'. What are the ethical implications? In short, is false documentary valid?

2. If *Hiroshima mon amour* is a false documentary (and why not?) then how do audiences react to it? What effect was it supposed to have? What effect does it actually have? If it's possible to *make* a false documentary that is valid (and both Resnais and Duras obviously thought so), then is it possible to *understand* a false documentary?

You can see, I'm sure, that we are already in the land of the philosophical conundrum. The first words of *Hiroshima* – very important words – are:

HE: You saw nothing in Hiroshima. Nothing.
SHE: I saw *everything. Everything.*[2]

During the last 18 years I have seen the film maybe half a dozen times and read the script, in French and in English, maybe another six times. I have yet to come to a conclusion about it – or rather I have come to two conclusions. At times, I see everything, at times, nothing. *Hiroshima* shifts like an optical paradox. Four years ago, preparing preliminary notes for this book, I was convinced that *Hiroshima mon amour* far from being a classic was at best an ambitious failure, beset and eventually overwhelmed by the paralysis which

3–2. Everything. Nothing.

haunts the characters within it. I thought its people were 'forced, allegorical, theme-ridden'. In her notes, Duras uses the phrase 'exemplary delusion of the mind'. Every other time I see it, *Hiroshima* appears to be caught in that paradox and destroyed by it.

Yet recently re-viewing the film I found this earlier dismissal itself superficial. In a way, Duras and Resnais have covered themselves perfectly. *Hiroshima* is a closed system, impervious to judgement. It feeds on its faults. You may not like it, but it doesn't matter in the least. Your reaction is the subject of the film, and its objective. Some of us see nothing in *Hiroshima*. Nothing. Others see *everything*. *Everything*. That is the point.

The theme of the film is the impossibility of making the film, a fact with which Resnais had had practical experience. Once this was established, the job of writing the script went surprisingly quickly. Duras conferred at every stage with both Resnais and Gérard Jarlot, who acted as literary adviser, never beginning a scene until both of them had commented upon the previous passage. The script was completed within two months. Resnais, for his part, shot the Japanese material in two months – August and September 1958 – and finished the French sequences by December of that year. It seems to have been quite easy to make a film about the impossibility of making a film.

Duras describes the significance of the first exchange between the two characters this way:

[It] is allegorical. *In short, an operatic exchange.* Impossible to talk about Hiroshima. All one can do is talk about the impossibility of talking about Hiroshima. The knowledge of Hiroshima being stated *a priori* by an exemplary delusion of the mind.

In order to emphasize this 'exemplary delusion' Duras intentionally sets up the dullest love story she can imagine: 'a banal tale, one that happens thousands of times every day'. It is to be hoped that the extraordinary contrast between the banality of the fiction and the outrage of the fact of Hiroshima will provide leverage to talk about talking about the subject. The title of the film condenses that contradiction. If it were translated into English it would be 'My Love Hiroshima', not 'Hiroshima, my love'. The two nouns are equivalent.

Neither of the characters are heroic in any way, and this was important, too, in order to set the mood. 'Their personal story,' Duras wrote in the introduction to the published screenplay, 'however brief it may be, always dominates Hiroshima'.

If this premise were not adhered to, this would be just one more made-to-order picture, of no more interest than any fictionalized documentary. If it is adhered to, we'll end up with a sort of false documentary that will probe the lesson of Hiroshima more deeply than any made-to-order documentary.

3–3. 'She', in costume for the film within the film, with her love Hiroshima: the banality of fiction

The device is a sort of aesthetic jiu-jitsu; instead of confronting the subject matter head on (and losing the contest), they will use its own strength against it. The banal love story has to dominate the enormity of the city's symbolic history.

Fully the first fifteen minutes of the film are given over to the documentary-that-never-was. On the soundtrack (dominating) we hear the conversations of the Japanese man and the French woman. The images are devoted to shots of Hiroshima now, and Hiroshima then. They are stark, dramatic, and harrowing. They bludgeon the viewer, as did the equally painful images of the death camps in 'Nuit et Brouillard', and their impact is doubled by the sallowness of the accompanying soundtrack which gives us a continuing groundbase of dull reality against which to measure the egregiousness of the bombing and its effects.

Having set up the history of the place, its private curse, Duras and Resnais need refer to it visually only occasionally throughout the film. It is fifteen minutes before we see the lovers' faces, but from that point on they dominate the image. Here begins the 'banal' love story. 'She' is French, an actress, about to finish her work on a film in Hiroshima about 'Peace' – not the film

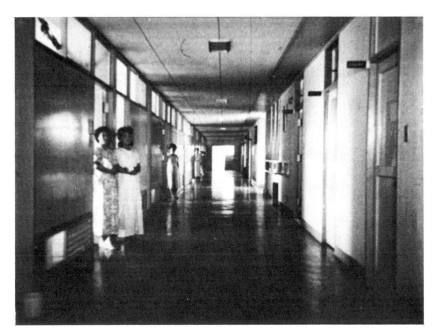

3–4. The documentary sequence: hospital corridors. Compare 4–2 (p. 55), 4–9 (p. 62), 7–1 (p. 121), 8–2 (p. 147), 9–22D (p. 188), and 10–9 (p. 199).

that wasn't made, but the one that never should have been; 'an enlightening film', as Duras describes it, 'not at all a ridiculous film, but just another film', 'He' is Japanese, but 'with a fairly "Western" face'. It is important that he not be interpreted by audiences as exotically Japanese because, although He and She are certainly allegorical, they must never appear so, else that would destroy the simplicity and banality of the love affair. It must not be thought that She was attracted to him explicitly because of his Japaneseness.

We join them in medias res. The time of the film lasts a little more than 24 hours, from late one evening until late the next. There is a passionate attraction on both their parts, but the affair is doomed to end when she returns to France. The drama of this thin plot (such as it is) involves her struggle to overcome her instincts and leave and his struggle to keep her there. Resnais and Duras have both speculated that maybe it does work out satisfactorily after the film is over. It couldn't matter less. The structure of the plot is a series of meetings: in her hotel room at night, on the set next day as it is being struck, at his house, at a bar the next evening, at the same bar later that night. At the same time as the interior dilemma of whether or not she will

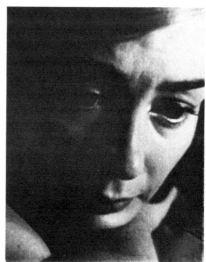

3–5–7. Riva's poses of personal memories punctuate the film. Here, three shots from the beginning, middle, and end. 5. She remembers her German lover's death. 6. She remembers Hiroshima. 7. In a mirror, 'I've betrayed you tonight with this stranger.' Connecting the two.

3–8, 9. Ground zero at the city hall – now 'Peace Square' – recalls the skylight arches of *Toute la mémoire du monde*. Different kinds of memories. Perhaps.

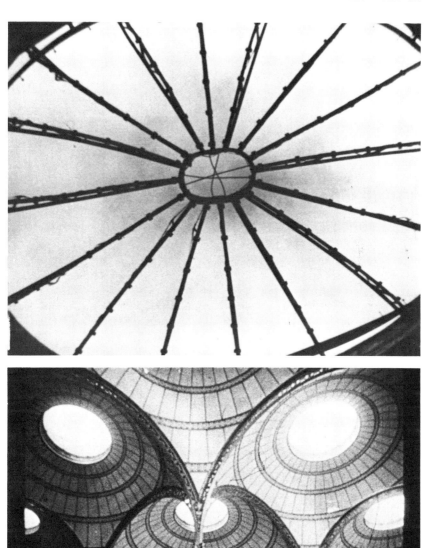

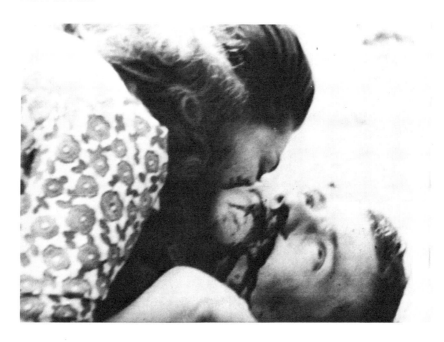

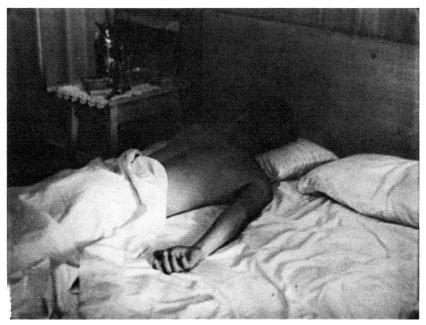

3–10, 11. 'You are dead ...' The memory of 3–5.

stay grows in intensity, the relationship between the two remains static. They are as involved in the beginning as they are in the end. It's a cyclical, static dance of death.

Couched within this love story (which takes up the major part of the film by far) are her memories of war, and his. His are global, disastrous, Hiroshiman (and at times identical with the first element of the film, the documentary). Hers are simple, personal, embarrassing – and at the same time more dramatic because on a more human scale. He remembers Hiroshima, She only Nevers. Nothing historical happened in Nevers.

In the obligatory and fairly lengthy French sequence She recalls her youth in Nevers at the end of the war. She fell in love with a German soldier. He was killed. She was sequestered in her parents' cellar, finally discovered, and given the standard punishment for women who consorted with German troops: her head was shaved. At the end of this memoire of personal humiliation, she leaves for Paris, never to return to Nevers.

The romances are necessarily contrasted and compared. Early in the film, as She looks at him, she flashes on a memory of the German as he lay dead. The postures of the two men are identical. Later, He asks her: 'When you are in the cellar, am I dead?'

Her response:

You are dead ... and ...
... How is it possible to bear such pain?
The cellar is very small.

Two painful, languorous romances. How is it possible?

Here we confront one of the major critical questions about *Hiroshima mon amour*. If *Hiroshima* seemed to be the insurmountable problem for Duras and Resnais, the solution, *mon amour*, may prove an even greater difficulty. Is 'false documentary' valid or effective?

In one direction it seems, on balance, to work quite well. The documentary shots, both present and past, of Hiroshima and all that it stands for are clearly heightened and protected against dismissal by the mundane background of the love story. The level of our response is conditioned by the banal saga of He and She which leaves us naked and open to the historical drama of the city, which is greater by so many magnitudes that it is immeasurable.

The problem reveals itself in the other direction, moving from Hiroshima to the love story. Since the latter supersedes the former on almost every level of the film, it is far too easy to read *Hiroshima mon amour* backwards, or inside out: as primarily a love story, one which uses Hiroshima and its history rather obscenely as background and filler to multiply the drama inherent in this supposedly intentionally banal story.

3–12–14. Romance in Nevers. Riva and Bernard Fresson.

Duras has faced the same dichotomous dilemma in nearly all the films she has directed herself in the last ten years. They are all at least skeletally love stories – universally banal – and moreover simplistically romantic. But of course, this is only the raw material. Duras's real work as an artist, her supporters will tell you, lies in the structural and material style of the films. What does the story matter when it's the telling not the tale which is the focus of creative energy?

Well, the story does matter. I think it is safe to conclude that *Hiroshima mon amour* received many of the accolades that it did not because it was a sophisticated 'false documentary' trying to deal with the question of the memory and history of Hiroshima, but rather because it was a poignant love story with a remarkable – even shocking – setting. For most viewers of the film, the tale wags the dog.

The distancing theory works perfectly in 'Nuit et Brouillard'. There is no way to misread that film because there is nothing in it but the subject. When fiction is added to the mix, however, it often becomes irresistible. Resnais was later to spend considerable effort investigating just this phenomenon, but *Hiroshima* is not an investigation, just an 'exemplary delusion of the mind': a fiction that uses history and to a great extent subsumes it.

In order to prevent the film from being read backwards, Resnais would have had to allow the documentary reality to dominate the fiction in some way. But Duras had set up the opposite relationship as the experiment. It is not surprising that the director and screenwriter discovered that more overtly political expressions didn't sit right in the mouths of their characters for they've invented lovers, not thinkers. Indeed, the energies of both characters are directed towards forgetting. Her aim, at the end of the film is to force him into oblivion: 'I'll forget you!' she screams at the end. 'I'm forgetting you already! Look how I'm forgetting you! Look at me!' Parting is such sweet sorrow.

And that brings us to the second caveat. If the film is actually being read and understood as a love story set in Hiroshima, even if it was made as a film about Hiroshima using the love story for leverage, then what does the love story tell us? He, in fact, is a rather shadowy character. His motivations aren't very clear, he doesn't have a chance to remember his own past in great detail (as She does), and the point of view of the story is clearly hers (and Duras's).

Her motivations are much more easily analysed. From the moment she flashes an image of the dead German soldier we have a good idea what fascinates her about him. It's not that he is Japanese; Duras and Resnais did protect themselves against that misreading. What is irresistible about him is that he is impossible. When He asks her to stay a few days longer, she replies:

Time enough for what? To live from it? To die from it?
HE: Time enough to know which.
SHE: That doesn't exist. Neither time enough to live from it. Nor time enough to die from it. So I don't give a damn.
HE: I would have preferred that you had died at Nevers.
SHE: So would I. But I didn't die at Nevers.

But she hasn't the courage to live. Not in Hiroshima. Probably not in Paris. Whatever the reasons for this death wish, it colours the whole relationship and eventually poisons it. She may not love him because he is Japanese, but she may very well owe her passion to the location of Hiroshima. Indeed, Duras announces that at the end of the film:

SHE: Hi-ro-shi-ma, Hi-ro-shi-ma. That's your name.

The conclusion we must draw is that the relationship is masochistic in the extreme. And maybe our own interest in Hiroshima – the film certainly, possibly the city, if not the event as well – is too.

That is not a good basis for an analysis of the memory and effect of the event of Hiroshima.

Yet there are a couple of tentative explanations for this structure of masochism. The script weakly suggests at one point that love among the ruins is a hopeful sign, like the ants that crawled out of the ashes to begin anew on the second day. Moreover, we can rest our case on the necessity of the tension

3-15-17. Pain in Nevers. 15. The remembered texture of the bare rock walls of the cellar. 16. The memory within the memory, of 17 the shame.

between the love story and the memory of horror: this is what, potentially, makes it possible to do an impossible film. We see the horror reflected in the love; the personal story serves as an index of history. We are prohibited from observing the thing itself, but the reduction gives us the scale of it. All this is true, ideally.

Consider, however, the way this relationship is set up. In the screenplay, Duras describes the opening sequence this way:

As the film opens, two pairs of bare shoulders appear, little by little. All we see are these shoulders – cut off from the body at the height of the head and hips – in an embrace, and as if drenched with ashes, rain, dew, or sweat, whichever is preferred. The main thing is that we get the feeling that this dew, this perspiration, has been deposited by the atomic 'mushroom' as it moves away and evaporates. It should produce a violent conflicting feeling of freshness and desire.

Here we can see the theory of the index, the bodies covered with the remains of the mushroom, which – like the filmmakers in the film – are always moving away, just out of reach. The abstract body parts certainly produce a striking image, yet precisely what is exciting about them is the frisson of the

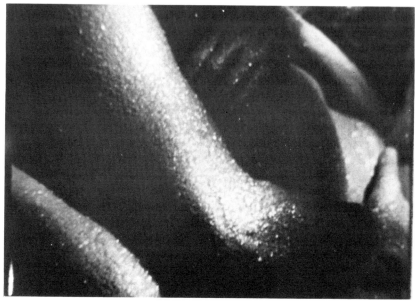

3.18 'drenched with ashes, rain, dew, or sweat ...'

juxtaposition of 'freshness and desire' and the deposit of the bomb.

Throughout the first documentary sequence of the film, as we survey the museum, the awful effects of the radiation, the banal streets of contemporary Hiroshima, and the newsreel and photographs of the event itself and the immediate aftermath – while we are trying to comprehend all this, we are forced to understand it in the context of the love scene which began the film and which continues in the person of Emmanuelle Riva's and Eiji Okada's voices on the soundtrack. In short, the horror of Hiroshima is part and parcel of their lovemaking.

In case we miss the connection, Duras has the woman deliver this monologue just before her face appears for the first time:

... I meet you.
I remember you.
Who are you?
You destroy me.
You're so good for me.
How could I have known that this city was made to the size of love?
How could I have known that you were made to the size of my body?
You're great. How wonderful. You're great.
How slow all of a sudden.
And how sweet.

More than you can know.
You destroy me.
You're so good for me.
You destroy me.
You're so good for me.
Plenty of time.
Please.
Take me.
Deform me, make me ugly.

With so much of this sort of sentiment lacing the dialogue of the film, it would be hard for audiences not to read it backwards. Yet, as I noted earlier, nothing is simple in *Hiroshima mon amour* – certainly not audience response.

The most useful key to a positive appreciation of this complex set of dichotomies and interferences lies with its images. We have been depending on the written script for evidence so far, and I think it's true that the script loses sight of the objective of the film. The neurotic love story comes through a lot more strongly than an attitude towards the meaning of Hiroshima. Insofar as audiences respond primarily to story line and dialogue, the film remains the kind of exploitative, morbid romance that it is just to call obscene. It's not a false documentary, it's documentedly false.

But Duras's script is not Resnais's film. The footage he has assembled for the factual sections is very nearly as shocking as the footage used in 'Nuit et Brouillard'. And the distancing effect works – at least, that is, until it becomes clear that the film is a love story, not a documentary. Moreover if on the soundtrack the lovers are morbidly and passionately paralysed, on screen the images of them Resnais has devised are direct, open, and active, and therefore contradictory. I think one can even see the explicit contrast between Duras's lovers and Resnais's in the stills reproduced here compared with the dialogue quoted. Visually, the film is exciting – even affirmative. From the intense, quick tracking shots which envelop us in the environment to the carefully composed portraits and medium shots which distance us from the plot, Resnais has with unusual aplomb for a first feature film, provided us with a subtext commentary: Hiroshima is what we should get into, the love story is what we should stay out of. Even for viewers who are not especially conscious of this visual irony, it has its effect.

Hiroshima mon amour then is two films, often working against each other. There is the fact of the place, and there is the fiction of the people. There is Japan, and there is France. There is the film for which Giovanni Fusco provided the music, and there is the one for which Georges Delerue did. There is the false documentary and the truly egregious love story. The film of images and the film of words.

3–19, 20. The tension between the two lovers at the end of the film is conveyed visually by images like these. They are rigidly posed, not facing each other, and the image has strong verticals. Compare 3–3 (p. 38) in which the diagonals dominate

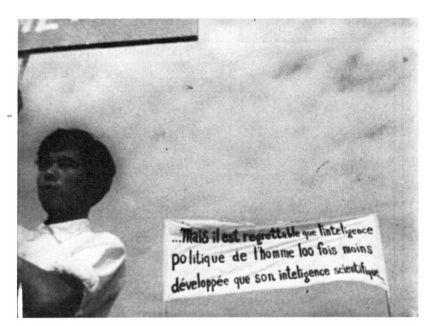

3–21. The film-within-the-film is not to be ignored. Here, the peace march which concludes it. '…But it is regrettable that man's political intelligence, 100 times less developed than his scientific intelligence…' 3–22. As time goes by.

I don't know whether Marguerite Duras knew what was going on when she saw the finished product. But I do think Alain Resnais knew what he was doing when he shot her script.

Here is an 'impossible' love story between two people struggling with the imagery of a distant war. At the end of this romantic, poignant movie about leavetakings and responsibilities, the two fateful lovers meet in a café. Resnais gives us a rare establishing shot of the location. 'He' is going to meet 'She' for the last time at a bar called 'The Casablanca' – right here in the middle of Hiroshima!

It's still the same old story. A fight for love and glory. A case of do or die. The world will always welcome lovers. As time goes by.

You must remember this: Alain Resnais has not quite found the right cinematic tone of voice for the work that lies ahead, but he is capable of reminding us and Marguerite Duras at the end of Hiroshima my darling that a kiss is still a kiss.

4. True Fiction

When it premiered at the Venice Film Festival in 1961, *L'Année dernière à Marienbad* (*Last Year at Marienbad*) created even more of a stir among progressive, educated audiences than had *Hiroshima mon amour* two years earlier. If *Hiroshima* was Resnais's debut excursion into the realm of sociopolitical significance, *Marienbad* took the directly opposite tack: towards pure style.* It was quickly recognized as a masterpiece of perceptual prestidigitation, and throughout the sixties served as the very model of the modern avant garde in narrative film, an honour it shared with Antonioni's *L'Avventura* during those years.

The minor revolution in the conventions of film language that both those films signalled so clearly had mainly to do with editing, or montage, and consequently with storytelling on the screen. The established Hollywood style of construction – *découpage classique* – had been refined during the thirty-year history of the sound film to the point where it was, in 1960, such an effective set of rules that it was nearly inviolable, which is why experiments like *L'Année dernière à Marienbad* appeared so strikingly innovative.

A kind of mundane, common-sense logic governs découpage classique. A sequence begins with an establishing shot, moves quickly to an intermediate shot conveying some useful information about the locale or characters, then concentrates on the triad of master shot, closeup, and reaction shot. The aim is to give the viewer as much information as possible, painlessly. 'Here is where we are,' the construction is saying in effect, 'here is what is happening. Now let's watch the people talk.' The master shot establishes the tight context of a dialogue. The closeup allows us to observe the emotions of

---

* Interestingly, Resnais's colleagues Truffaut and Godard also began their careers with pairs of films so opposite in style that they served to stake out the limits of their areas of interest. *Les Quatre Cents Coups* and *A Bout de souffle* were both essentially realistic, with a sociopolitical tinge, while *Tirez sur le pianiste* and *Une Femme est une femme* – like *Marienbad* – had more to do with movies than with life and were appositely, exercises in style.

4–1, 2. 'Structural flashbacks.' Compare 3–8, 3–9 (p. 41), 3–4 (p. 39), and 2–15 (p. 24). Establishing the space.

the speaker; and the reaction shot serves similarly for the listener. Occasionally, detail shots provide necessary information that can't be communicated verbally. The Hollywood style, with admirable precision, creates a seamless flow of time and story that moves effortlessly through the classic dramatic construction from introduction to elaboration to climax to aftermath to conclusion. The goal is to have the greatest sum effect on audiences, and image is almost always subordinate to dialogue, where, after all, the real story is happening.

Establish, move in, explain, speaker, listener, speaker, listener, speaker. The pattern repeats itself with lulling rhythms to create a great sense of security. As D. W. Griffith himself explained it, this system simply visualized the patterns of attention which had already been established during the great age of the novel in the last century, and this mode of storytelling with its admirable and thoroughly practical clarity is still dominant in both popular literature and film: establish, describe, listen to the dialogue. And then what happened? And *then*?

But Resnais, like numerous other filmmakers of the early sixties, had lost patience with what seemed to be a mode that was dominant mainly because it was eminently prosaic. Découpage classique presented reality well enough, but only one kind of it. One of the main problems with the style was tense. Film *is*: the present tense rules. The past tense (and less often the future) could be communicated by means of the code of the dissolve, but the conditional was considerably more difficult. In découpage classique, it was

nearly impossible to picture what had not happened and, indeed, even the simple past tense usually needed the reinforcement of accompanying narration. The spoken language was necessary to explain in what temporal context the image had to be viewed. Most of the twentieth-century stylistic innovations of the novel were therefore unavailable to découpage classique: stream of consciousness, multiple points of view, and other formal codes were strictly alien to the dominant mode of film discourse Hollywood had created and established.

What Resnais and the generation of the sixties had to do was to free film discourse from this dependence on dialogue as the governing element of the cinematic formula. The new object was to tell stories in images rather than words and in this respect, the innovators of the sixties often returned to the conventions of the silent film for models. Resnais said of *Marienbad*,

I wanted to renew a certain style of the silent cinema. The direction and the make-up try to recreate this atmosphere.[1]

He even went so far as to ask Eastman Kodak to supply an old-fashioned filmstock that would 'bloom' or 'halo'. (They couldn't do it.)

What Resnais and Alain Robbe-Grillet did in *Marienbad* that appeared so strikingly avant-garde in 1961 was, essentially, to simplify the mode of discourse. The rules of découpage classique were ignored: each image existed for itself and could be understood in the context of its surrounding images and the general narrative line in a variety of ways. Resnais had experimented

4–3. X and A on the dance floor. 'I wanted to renew a certain style of the silent cinema'

cautiously with several of these techniques in *Hiroshima*, but the innovations there were minimal. (Of *Hiroshima*, he said: 'Personally, I thought I had made an "old-fashioned" film, in the style of 1930, with experiments in editing and cutting.'[2]) The opening sequence, in which the love scene is juxtaposed with the documentary footage and the poetic monologue is probably the most adventurous of these experiments, but throughout the film establishing shots are eschewed. Now that we are thoroughly accustomed to this technique it doesn't appear at all remarkable, but it must have seemed more striking to contemporary viewers in 1959.

Marienbad, however, is solidly grounded in the new syntax. It's the basic premise for the film. The classic sequence of establishing and closeup shots appears only by accident in the film. Moreover, any particular shot can be read as either present tense, past tense, conditional or subjunctive, or pure fantasy. This too is realism, but of a quite different sort from the prosaic Hollywood kind. Robbe-Grillet called it 'mental realism', but we understand it most simply as the kind of interior monologue we are used to from contemporary novels. Just to show how cautious this new syntax really is, Robbe-Grillet depends heavily on a spoken narration. We know from the beginning of the film that 'X' is telling this story, that it is a kind of stream of consciousness, and that whatever happens must be understood through the filtering persona of X. No one has any trouble with this kind of first person narration in prose. Approached without preconceptions, *Marienbad* should be just as easily comprehended.*

After the success of *Hiroshima mon amour* Resnais was in demand. In 1959 and early 1960 he considered a number of varying projects. According to Roy Armes these included Daniel Anselme's novel *La Permission* and a script for a film to be called 'A Suivre à n'en plus finir', written by Anne-Marie de Villaine, which was to have dealt with the Algerian War in the context of the relationship of a young couple. There was also Jean Cayrol's *Muriel, ou le temps d'un retour*, the work on which had begun before Resnais even met Alain Robbe-Grillet.

Resnais claims he was unfamiliar with Robbe-Grillet's novels before they began work on the scenario of *L'Année dernière à Marienbad*, but being conversant with literary trends he certainly must have understood in broad outline what the 'nouveau roman' was up to and how his attitudes and Robbe-Grillet's could coincide. The impetus for the project belonged to the producers, Raymond Froment and Pierre Courau, who brought the author and the auteur together in the early winter of 1960. The work on the script proceeded quickly. Robbe-Grillet, already with plans of his own to direct films, wrote out a lengthy scenario which Resnais changed very little. Of all his films, this one was least an intense collaboration between writer and director. Resnais limited himself to only occasional comments and, once the film began shooting, Robbe-Grillet was busy elsewhere (in Turkey, preparing what was to be his own debut as director, *L'Immortelle*). In his introduction to the published script, Robbe-Grillet claims that he and Resnais had originally planned to co-sign the film without indicating who had done the writing, who the directing, but in light of the apparent tensions between script and *mise en scène*, it seems likely that this was more wishful thinking on the part of the scenarist than a solid agreement based on a mutuality of interests. Indeed, Robbe-Grillet's published reactions to the film are unpleasantly snide.

Robbe-Grillet, with very little input from Resnais, produced a detailed if eccentrically phrased shooting script which included precise descriptions of

---

* Resnais's innovation in *Marienbad* involved different levels of tense. In *L'Avventura*, Antonioni experimented with duration within the present tense, equally important for contemporary cinema. Instead of cutting just after the meaning of the scene had been comprehended, he allowed it to run on into 'dead time' which was thematically meaningful rather than narratively significant. Resnais's experiments were on the vertical axis of film time, Antonioni's along the horizontal axis.

4–4, 5. Narration in *Marienbad*: 4. Multiplex images: one single reflection and three double reflections of Delphine Seyrig, but not Seyrig herself. 5. Stage perspective: Seyrig in her room, as in 4, but seen from a low angle, as if on a stage.

shots, editing, even music. At first, Resnais seemed to feel constrained by this rigorous plan, but once shooting began, he says, he discovered an unusual freedom within the imposed discipline of the elaborate script. This is no doubt one of the major reasons he has worked so closely with screenwriters since to produce a meticulous screenplay before shooting and has improvised so little on the set. *Marienbad* was shot on location in Munich, at Nymphenburg, Schleissheim, and other chateaux, and at

4–6. X and A confront the puzzle of the chateau

Phonosonor studios, Paris, during September, October, and November 1960. When Robbe-Grillet finally saw the finished product he remarked upon both how closely Resnais had realized his own intentions and how utterly different everything was.

The elegant puzzle Robbe-Grillet had designed and Resnais had executed is this: X (Giorgio Albertazzi) is telling us a story. We are at the spa Marienbad. A year ago X had met A (Delphine Seyrig) at Marienbad or at a spa very much like it. A was (and is) with M (Sacha Pitoëff) who may be her husband. X had an affair with her. Now he thinks he has met her again. But she denies the previous meeting. So X spends the course of the film trying to convince her that it existed. Or that it exists. Or that it will exist. Or that it should have or should now or should in the future exist. At the end, the drama begins all over again. Clearly, this happens outside of time, or at least without reference to it. It doesn't matter in the slightest whether X is right (that they did meet) or that A is right (that they didn't), it only matters that X is trying to convince A that his story is the truth.

If *Hiroshima* was a 'false documentary', then *Marienbad* is a 'true fiction'. In other words, it is about storytelling. It is X's job to convince, A's job to resist: the primal relationship between storyteller and audience. From this point of view, *L'Année dernière* is an essay in aesthetics and Marienbad is the 'House of Fiction' that was to fascinate Jacques Rivette in films such as *Out One* and *Céline et Julie vont en bateau* several years later. In the Pirandellian tradition, the 'truth', 'reality' is beside the point. There is a material reality to cinema which is irresistible: what you see is what you get.

But beyond that practical level, narratives or stories are equally valid and veristic. It is not that all stories are illusions (which is the way Pirandello's theory is usually simplistically interpreted) but that all stories are truths of a kind. There is simply no way to evaluate one as more or less valid than another.

4–7, 8. The fictional setting of *Marienbad*. Giorgio Albertazzi and Delphine Seyrig bracket a strongly framed image of the garden, Sacha Pitoëff intrudes between them in another shot as they frame a trompe l'oeil courtyard.

This startling material truth of cinema is apparently what attracted Robbe-Grillet to the medium in the first place. As a practitioner of the 'nouveau roman' in the fifties he had been involved in an aesthetic struggle to clear away the underbrush of opinion from the landscape of the novel, to give it a greater material validity than it had had in the past. One way to do this was to outlaw differences in tense. Then the truth of memory or fiction (past tense) would be equal to the truth of experience (present tense) which in turn would be equal to the truth of fantasy, logical extrapolation, and invention (future and conditional tenses). This is what would happen to time in the new novel Robbe-Grillet conceived. In *For a New Novel* (1963) he described what would happen to space:

In this novelistic world of the future, gestures and objects will be 'there' before being 'something'; and they will still be there after, strong, inalterable, present for ever....

In short, the materials of the novel are now subject to the tenets of the philosophy of Materialism. Everything is present. And everything in the present has existence before it has significance. Describing a similar universe in his own films, Jacques Rivette once explained, 'nothing takes place but the place'. This is the world of *Marienbad*: no differences in degrees of validity between past, present, and future; no meaning without existence. 'A stone is a better pillow than many visions,' Wallace Stevens put it.

Now obviously, this fictional universe intends to be measurably more concrete than its predecessor. Paradoxically, it is experienced however as more abstract. Because it is theoretical, it requires a certain effort on the part of the observer. Or rather it doesn't, but it appears as if it does. Children, no doubt, without the baggage of knowledge of the elaborate conventions of storytelling would be able to comprehend a narrative like *Marienbad* a lot more quickly than adults who have to struggle at every turn to remind themselves that the old rules, so ingrained in literary and cinematic sensibility, are no longer operative.

Despite all this, much of *Marienbad* is crystal clear and in fact can be understood in the old way. An experiment it may be, but it is a conservative one. For the most part, it doesn't matter whether we understand Robbe-Grillet's theories or not. The image of Marienbad: ornate, baroque, stylized, is interesting for itself as pure setting. Moreover, there is a plot, contrary to popular belief. The relationship between X and M, for example, if examined in isolation, is no different from what we might expect in an ambitious Hollywood film. They play a macho game that is nevertheless civilized (in the sense of utilizing upper-class manners). The struggle for A's affections takes place here and now and the main metaphor for it is the match game which

4–9. This is the famous shot from the film which was widely reprinted in publicity materials. The people are 'there' and 'something'. They cast shadows. The manicured trees and statues are merely 'there'. No shadows

M and X engage in several times during the course of the film. In addition, the M-X-A relationships are set in the context of the large group of other guests, none of whom has to deal with the persuasions of the main narrative. They are hazily outlined, but they know a battle is going on between X and M (and X and A) and they react to it the same way we might expect them to. XMA is a minor scandal at a dull resort and therefore one of the main entertainments.

In case we miss the point, Robbe-Grillet begins the film and ends it with quick scenes in the resort theatre. The inference is unmistakable: the play's the thing, whether we watch it on the little stage, or on the dance floor, in the lounges or in the gardens of Marienbad.

This *petit drâme* is communicated to us on several levels of discourse: the materialism of the film is perhaps primary, but at various times during the film we also have to comprehend the story in terms of basic human drama (as the other guests do), as an essay on the new novel and the new film, as a study of persuasion (which relates both to the essay and the drama), as a mathematical game (the abstract personal pronouns of Hiroshima have been reduced to the algebraic quantities A, M, and X), and, finally, as a straight sexual fantasy of the type that Robbe-Grillet soon was to become obsessed with in the films he directed himself.

The quality which more than anything else sets *Marienbad* apart is its

4–10, 11. Games and rituals: 10. A fourteen-pipped card on the table between hazy reflections of X and M. 11. X and M in one of their several confrontations over the 'match game'

materialism. Robbe-Grillet writes that what attracted him to Resnais's work was 'the uncompromising rigour of its composition'.

> In it I recognized my own efforts toward a somewhat ritual deliberation, a certain slowness, a sense of the theatrical, even that occasional rigidity of attitude, that hieratic quality in gesture, word and setting which suggests both a statue and an opera.[3]

Marienbad is a magnificently tactile film: an opera of statues. The key image here is the one reproduced on p. 62 which became the chief advertising image for the film: the people are sculptural volumes, masses, to be manipulated like the statues which populate the endless gardens. The first sequence of the film begins the lengthy catalogue of architectural details which provides the main trope of the film and which continues through innumerable doors, mirrors, pillars, stairs, halls, rooms, gardens, pictures, lamps, balustrades, bannisters, tables, chairs, posts, chandeliers, draperies, paintings, and even an occasional window.

Here is X's monologue which accompanies the majestic tracking shots in the first sequence:

> Once again – I walk on, once again, down these corridors, through these halls, these galleries, in this structure – of another century, this enormous, luxurious, baroque, lugubrious hotel – where corridors succeed endless corridors – silent, deserted corridors overloaded with a dim, cold ornamentation of woodwork, stucco, mouldings, marble, black mirrors, dark paintings, columns, heavy hangings – sculptured door frames, series of doorways, galleries – transverse corridors that open in turn on empty salons, rooms overloaded with an ornamentation from another century, silent halls where the sound of advancing footsteps is absorbed by carpets so thick and heavy that nothing can be heard, as if the ear of the man walking on once again, down these corridors – through these halls, these galleries, in this structure of another century, this enormous, luxurious, baroque, lugubrious hotel –[4]

This reptilian sentence continues for another dozen or fourteen lines in the same manner but even in this translation one can see that Robbe-Grillet is fabricating an order of prose that is peculiarly French (and doesn't really work all that well in English). Orotund, heavily periodic, looming, lugubrious itself, it mocks the basic style of the film and announces immediately that there is an element of irony that cannot be discounted. Because it comes across so poorly in English (especially in subtitles that have space to translate so little of it) I think English-speaking audiences were relatively immune to this important aspect of *L'Année dernière à Marienbad*. Both Resnais and Robbe-Grillet take distinct pleasure in this 'ritual deliberation', this 'hieratic quality' which verges perilously close to camp. It may be of a fineness that is not quickly appreciated, but there is honest humour here.

The humour – a droll irony – is redoubled in the images, not only in this sequence, but throughout the film. The tone of the images might not be so apparent in shots of the architecture, decor, and landscaping, but it is obvious in the stylized poses of the close-ups and group shots. A number of them are *trompe l'oeil* effects (see p. 62). Always, the people of *L'Année dernière* pose, rather than simply stand, talk, or look. The exaggerated quality is reminiscent of the silent film style Resnais means to evoke, and it makes it clear that the people are material of composition just as the elements of

4–12. 'Silent halls where the sound of advancing footsteps. . . .' X is looking directly at A but we can't see her and the images of the two are separated by the baroque frame. The 'mirrored hallway' is a double trope here

4–13. Pitoëff, the vampire figure, poses in front of the chateau

decors are, but the posing also has sociological roots – in the theory of *sprezzatura* that was so popular in the Renaissance: a mode of posing that is particularly associated with ruling-class behaviour.

Note, too, that the elaborate poses of *Marienbad* are very much a function of X's narrative. Giorgio Albertazzi is clearly the most natural and unaffected of the trio, as befits a man seen from his own point of view, while Sacha Pitoëff cuts a lugubrious figure which is by turns comical and vicious. It reminds us that vampire psychology underlies the film.

Most of the poses, however, are lavished on Delphine Seyrig. As an actress, she is perfectly capable of naturalistic style, as evidenced by her first film, Robert Frank's *Pull My Daisy* (1958) and one of her most recent, Chantal Akerman's *Jeanne Dielman, 23 Quai du Commerce, 1080 Bruxelles* (1976). But throughout most of her career she has been haunted by the stylization of *Marienbad*, her first major role. She is, as David Thomson has noted, 'a Proustian actress in the way she is able to invest small gestures with an enormous imaginary train'.[5] She is essential to the iconography of *L'Année dernière à Marienbad*.

Through most of the film, what we see on the screen is simply an illustration of X's narration. The break into human drama which comes near the end when M confronts A in their room about X is thus all the more striking, like coming out of the dream into waking for the first time.

The seed for the confrontation is a photograph of A taken last year.

M: Oh? (pause) Who took it
A: I don't know ... Frank, perhaps ...
M: Last year, Frank wasn't here ...

(Frank, by the way, is X's name within the story X is telling. It most often comes out in talk about last year by the other characters.)

X took the picture. It is X's best proof that the story he tells is the truth. Pictures, including moving ones, don't lie. This is Robbe-Grillet's axiom:

No doubt the cinema is the preordained means of expression for a story of this kind. The essential characteristic of the image is its presentness. Whereas literature has a whole gamut of grammatical tenses which make it possible to narrate events in relation to each other, one might say that on the screen verbs are always in the present tense....by its nature, what we see on the screen *is in the act of happening*, we are given the gesture itself, not an account of it.[6]

The human drama is the most minor element of the total equation for *L'Année dernière à Marienbad*. This scene, the most naturalistically dramatic in the film, segues quickly into a commentary on the new narrative form. When compared with similar films, it is even more apparent that the drama here is obligatory rather than felt. Take Bergman's *The Silence*, made three

4–14–16. Seyrig's poses: 14. Off-centre in the converging perspective. The trees have shadows now, stronger than A's. 15 and 16. A has a particular fondness for doorways, where she can be between rooms, between places. The hand is always to the throat in a protective, nervous gesture. 15: last year. 16: this year. Or: the other way around.

years later. It is also a harsh, dreamlike narrative set in a hotel with intricate networks of corridors, but never once in *The Silence*, despite the similarities of setting and mood, does the attention stray from psychological drama.

As a narrative game with mathematical proportions, *Marienbad* excites some interest. Many commentators have attempted to solve the equation

4–17. 'Who took it?' 'Frank, perhaps.' A examines photograph which she holds within a book. The words are as useful as the image. They lie as well, too

4–18. A in happier times (last year), just before the photo was taken

4–19. The imprisoned princess during the confrontation scene

Robbe-Grillet has taken such pains to construct and much of what has been written about the film deals with it in this chosen metaphor.

Gaston Bounoure, for example, uses the calculus, and introduces differentials. For Bounoure, $dA = a$ patient (in support he offers Resnais's suggestion that 'perhaps this hotel isn't anything but a clinic'.), $dX =$ death (he suggests that we go back to Breton myths to understand the structure of the film. In those myths, death often comes searching for victims after having permitted them a year's grace.), and $dM = a$ fairy king, who has kept the princess imprisoned waiting for her Prince Charming. There are also the mathematical possibilities that $A + X + M = 1$ and $A + X + M = 0$, that is that each of the characters is a facet of the same personality, or that none of them exist at all. But most of this sort of analysis is specious. It focuses on the characters, as if they were central to the film, and they are not.

There are two aspects to *Marienbad*, nevertheless, which have to do with very human qualities even if they are not expressed in character, but rather in style. For Robbe-Grillet:

The whole film, as a matter of fact, is the story of a persuasion: it deals with a reality which the hero creates out of his own vision, out of his own words. And if his persistence, his secret conviction, finally prevail, they do so among a perfect labyrinth of false trails, variants, failures, and repetitions![7]

Marienbad is a love story of sorts, a seduction, but not primarily of one character by another. The author of *In the Labyrinth* is alluding in the passage above to his own attempted seduction of us. His own personal fantasies, if we are to judge from the films he has made, verge on the sadomasochistic, and there are elements of that here. A, near the end of the film, fantasizes rape, murder, and suicide – never in as explicit detail as Robbe-Grillet will later apply in his own films, but there nevertheless, and audiences may respond.

This leads us to a discussion of the ethics of the New Cinema, of which *L'Année dernière à Marienbad* is an early and important example. Since tense doesn't apply in this film neither does memory. It is not about what X remembers, what A remembers, what M recalls, but about what one Alain tells us through the mouth of X, and what the other Alain does to shape what the first tells us. The operating axis is not character–character, but author–spectator.

Resnais himself seems not to have been entirely pleased with Robbe-Grillet's sexual/technical/narrative fantasy. 'There was a time during the preparation of *Marienbad*,' he says,

when I would arrive with my little black notebook and propose to Robbe-Grillet, for example, making the real world intervene in the form of conversations about a political problem that seemed insoluble, at least to those having the conversations.

4–20. X persuades A in words and gesture, but A is clearly seducing X, as well

4-21. 'Totally dreamlike.' The reality of the spectre: the washed out image of A in her feather negligee.

None of those solutions worked in the context of the film, and Resnais gradually came around to the point of view that

it was the spectators themselves who, when they saw the film, would naturally represent the real world and that it was therefore impossible to include them in advance inside the film.[8]

There's something a little self-serving about this conclusion. At this stage of the 'New Film' there was no reason not to include the reality of the spectator inside the film and to do so would have made it more immediately perceivable if less profitably mysterious. Yet, it's undoubtedly true that *Marienbad*'s most important accomplishment is its shift of attention from the character axis to the author–observer axis. This implies that the observer has to work to complete the film. He must be an active participant. It is the strongest contradiction of Hollywood's *découpage classique*, in which it was taken for granted that the sole aim of cinema was to do as much as possible for the observer. Interestingly, it is in such a dreamplay as *Marienbad* that the viewer is freed from having his dreams provided for him by the film-makers.

The ethical ramifications of this are eventually profoundly important in terms of the politics of film, as Jean-Luc Godard would demonstrate later in the sixties. If Hollywood (or Paris or Cinecittà) dreams for us we can't dream for ourselves. If we can't dream for ourselves we have no ideal to oppose to the reality that surrounds us and the function of culture becomes reinforcement rather than criticism of the established order.

Resnais, I think, had a strong feeling for this ethic. I'm not sure Robbe-Grillet did. From everything he has written about his experience with *L'Année dernière à Marienbad* it seems as if this new axis was valuable to him solely for its aesthetic possibilities rather than for what it meant in terms of renewing relationships between the producers of culture and the consumers.

In general, it may have been a mistake for Resnais to shoot his first two feature films from scripts by avant-garde novelists. As an art form, the novel was past middle-age, well into its nonage. Such aesthetic experimentation had become almost a necessity, at least for those artists who wanted a place in the history of the form. But film was still just past adolescence. Resnais's own concerns which parallel those of Duras and Robbe-Grillet might well have been better expressed in films which had a fresher, more naive, less heavily theoretical provenance. The early work of Godard and Truffaut comes to mind. 'False documentary', true fiction', the process of narrative, the materialism of the image, the function of memory, even the self-consciousness of an art which had become self-conscious about itself because it had developed a sense of its own history and an active intelligence about its own theory were just as well covered in such films as *A bout de souffle*, *Les Quatre Cents Coups*, *La Femme mariée*, and *Tirez sur le pianiste* as in the more lugubrious films with which Resnais began. Paradoxically, it was this artificial seriousness which assured his place in the new pantheon of film – not to the good, I think.

4-22. 'It seemed impossible to lose one's way there.' The last image of the film.

Resnais himself seems to have had misgivings about this. 'Yes, *L'Année dernière à Marienbad* is totally dreamlike,' he admitted shortly after it had been completed. 'It's a musical comedy, without songs, that tries to deepen the forces of revery.'[9]

In his next film, he'd add the songs.

5. Bad Memories

In *Muriel, ou le temps d'un retour* everything comes together for Alain Resnais, and the experiments of the first two feature films pay off. *Muriel* shares with its predecessors a fascination with the phenomenon of memory and imagination; and like *Hiroshima* and *Marienbad* it situates its examination of the world of the mind in a geographical place which has its own concrete significance and which serves, in addition, as the locus for states of mind. But it is notable that the title of this, Resnais's third feature, is not as the previous pattern would indicate, 'Boulogne'. *Muriel* is named for a person, not a place; for the first time Resnais finds a cinematic key that allows a human and deeply-felt emotional dimension. Characters are no longer identified by pronouns and algebraic symbols; they're allowed to live. They are liberated for the first time, no longer plot- and theme-ridden but free to 'do things we don't approve of'.

The shock of events is nearly as strong here in Boulogne as it was in Hiroshima, and the design of the film is structurally just as sophisticated (and for some confusing) as in *Marienbad*, but there is a new resonance in *Muriel* that brings the film sharply alive. The intellectual puzzles of the earlier features pale in comparison. Memory and the power of imagination are central here too, and are used as weapons against oneself and against others, but now we see this theory in a practical, vital context of everyday life.

Certainly the major reason *Muriel* is measureably more successful than the two films which first established Resnais's reputation as an influential director is the quality of his relationship with the screenwriter. Eleven years older than Resnais, Jean Cayrol had been a good friend for many years. He was, of course, the author of the text for Resnais's most important short film, 'Nuit et Brouillard', the basic metaphor of which was owed to an early Cayrol volume of poetry, *Poèmes de la nuit et du brouillard* (1945). For years, he and Resnais had planned to make a feature together. At one point it looked as if Resnais

5-1. Hélène Aughain lives on the thin edge. In this, one of the earliest shots of the film, she over-reacts to some minor disturbance.

had raised the money to film one of Cayrol's novels but the project fell through when Resnais was face to face with the artistic difficulties involved in translating one art form into another. Roy Armes reports that Resnais, Cayrol, and Chris Marker had planned at one point to film the life of Christ together, but that too was added to the long list of unrealized projects.

Cayrol's and Resnais's own interests neatly dovetailed. Cayrol had been an inmate of the death camps during the war and had suffered bouts of amnesia. No wonder, then, that his work has been coloured by an obsession with memory and the relationship of past life with present. More importantly, he saw memory in precisely the way Resnais did, as an alternate reality, equal in value to present experience, rather than more simplistically as a frozen record. 'Muriel', after all is a real person, but one we never see in the film (only in the film within the film). She is the construction of Bernard's imagination, although none the less real for it.

Cayrol and Resnais first talked of the project of *Muriel* in 1959. Resnais didn't begin shooting until three years later (the film was shot between November 1962 and January 1963) and the long drawn-out dialectical process of the development of the screenplay became a model for Resnais's later films. Cayrol provided a lot more information than appears in the published version of the screenplay (*Muriel*, by the way, is one of two Resnais features not available in English) so that the director could develop a feel for the characters' pasts and idiosyncrasies at the same time as he had the freedom to make choices between one version of a scene and another. This pattern was also followed for the later films.

Although *Muriel* has a highly complex montage, very little of it was developed during and after shooting. Cayrol himself had ambitions to make films and had directed a series of shorts beginning with 'On vous parle' (1960). Later, he was to direct a couple of features as well. He knew and was fascinated with the routine of the editing room (another point of comparison between him and Resnais) so that nearly all the complex montages of *Muriel* appear outlined in the shooting script.

Despite the fact that it is much more lively, quicker paced, expansive, allusive, and vital than either *Hiroshima* or *Marienbad*, *Muriel* has an equally elaborate and sophisticated structure. Resnais didn't abandon his stylistic interests of the earlier films, he simply put them in the service of a richer and more meaningful film. Cayrol, in the published script, sets up a five act structure. All the action of the film takes place in Boulogne-sur-mer between Saturday, 29 September 1962 and Sunday, 14 October of that year. The first and fifth acts each cover one day, the second and fourth a week each, and the third 2 days precisely in the middle of the time span. Three meals provide focal points at beginning, middle, and end. Different sections are mainly devoted to different characters. In short, *Muriel* has an elegant plan, yet none of this is at all noticeable on the screen since the structure does not force the cinematic material, it underlines it. This is the essential difference between *Muriel* and the films that had come before it.

Resnais himself seems to have been uneasy with the more elaborate stylistic concerns which Duras and Robbe-Grillet had imposed on *Hiroshima* and *Marienbad*. He was exhilarated when Cayrol's script gave him a chance at last to move into the fresh air of the real world, as it were, and this emotion permeates the film. The people of the film are essentially no more interesting or likeable than He, She, X, A, and M, but they have room to breathe. 'The place takes place', here, but the people take action, too.

Finally, the film has a relevant political dimension as no film of Resnais's since 'Nuit et Brouillard' seven years earlier had had. *Hiroshima mon amour* doesn't count as a political statement since its concerns are so broad. The only conclusion to be drawn from it is that war is hell and the bomb was horrible. *Muriel*, on the other hand, investigates a current, specific problem and expresses it in terms of personal action. The early sixties was the time of the terrorist bombing campaign of the O.A.S. (Secret Army Organization) in France, which had as its aim the resubjugation of Algeria. Bernard, who

5–2. Hélène meets her courtly remembered lover Alphonse at the station, but she is late. She has misremembered the schedule

becomes progressively more important than his mother Hélène throughout the course of the film until he completely dominates it at the end, is in the process of coming to grips with his own responsibility for the Algerian war. The title of the film announces that this is the ultimate subject of the film, since 'Muriel' is the personification of Bernard's responsibility. If it is argued that the political materials seem subdued, it must be remembered that the pervasive anxiety was much more apparent to French audiences at the time the film was released. Watching the film now we must continually remind ourselves of it. Moreover, the censorship situation clearly prohibited any more direct statement. Godard's second film, *Le Petit Soldat*, also dealt with the Algerian situation, although in a much more oblique and, in the end, muddled way. It was banned for several years. A film not shown is a film without effect.

Since the intricate fabric Cayrol weaves is such an important part of the sum effect of *Muriel*, it seems worthwhile to summarize the plot of the film in some detail.

Hélène Aughain (Delphine Seyrig) lives with her stepson Bernard in

Boulogne where she makes a living selling more or less antique furniture from her flat. Her current lover is Roland de Smoke (Claude Sainval) with whom she spends most of her time at the casino. She is a compulsive gambler. De Smoke is not particularly important to her during the fortnight of the film. None of her Boulogne friends are, except possibly Claudie (Laurence Badie), for as the film begins she is nervously awaiting a visit from a man she knew

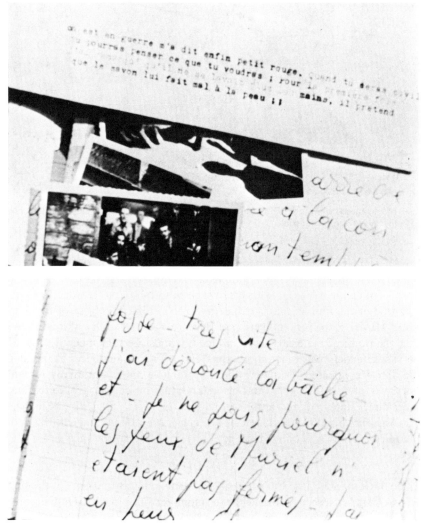

5-3-5. Bernard's 'evidence': letters, snapshots, diaries, notes, and harsh, grainy, 8-mm film

during the war, Alphonse Noyard (Jean-Pierre Kerien). She thinks – she remembers – that she was in love with him. Alphonse arrives with Françoise (Nita Klein) who, he says, is his neice. She is actually his mistress.

Bernard (Jean-Baptiste Thierrée) has recently returned from Army service in Algeria. We gradually learn that he is obsessed with the experience, especially an episode of torture in which a young Algerian girl died. He has named her 'Muriel'. He blames his friend Robert (Philippe Laudenbach) for the death. He spends most of his time in his workroom in the old section of the city poring over 8-mm films taken in Algeria, talking, and making love with Marie-Do (Martine Vatel), the one character in the film who is more interested in her future than her past. She plans to go to Argentina for three years.

We know none of this as the film begins. Cayrol and Resnais eschew all exposition; audiences are thrown into the middle of things. We see Hélène dealing with clients. Bernard leaves for his workroom (as he often does during the course of the film). Hélène goes to the station to meet Alphonse. He arrives with Françoise, but what relationship does she have with him? It only becomes clear later. They walk home through the darkened city. Bernard returns and the four of them eat the dinner that Hélène has cooked. Bernard and Françoise go out leaving Alphonse and Héléne to talk and only now does it become apparent what their relationship has been. Alphonse makes a pass, which is rejected. He starts to tell a story about a girl he knew during the war. Hélène interrupts him: 'But, that's our story!' she exclaims. Roland de Smoke arrives. Strangely, Hélène goes out with him, leaving her just-arrived guest alone. Alphonse is annoyed, spends the evening looking in drawers, searching desks, opening doors, and reading Bernard's diary. Hélène and Roland have gone to the casino. She has lost again. Françoise wanders

5-6-9. Resnais gives us portraits of the major characters early on: four quick shots of the four during their first conversation. Hélène, Bernard, Françoise, Alphonse.

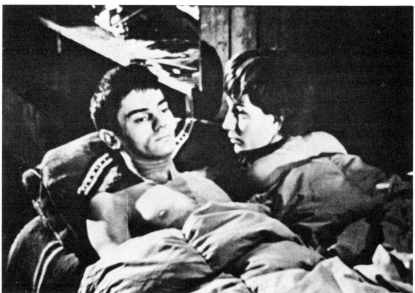

5–10. Bernard on his horse, early in the morning
5–11. Bernard and Marie-Do in his workshop

5–12. Ernest (Jean Champion) makes his first appearance
5–13. Alphonse, de Smoke, Françoise, Hélène lost in the same room together. Hélène looks nervously across de Smoke and Françoise to Alphonse on the phone

around the city. Later that night, Hélène, Françoise and Bernard all wander in at different times.

The 'second act', like the fourth, is even more fragmented than the focal points of the first, third, and fifth acts. We get information piecemeal. Bernard says 'I'm not making films, I'm collecting evidence!' The relationship – or memory of it – between Alphonse and Hélène further deteriorates, but Alphonse refuses to leave. Bernard rides a white horse on the cliffs by the sea early in the morning. A new character, Ernest (Jean Champion), makes inquiries about Alphonse. Marie-Do is leaving for Argentina. Françoise has decided to break up with Alphonse once they return to Paris.

A typical sequence in the middle part of the film runs like this: Shots of shop windows....Alphonse and Françoise are walking, separately....Quick montage: day, night in the city....Françoise....Day....Bernard, Hélène, and Alphonse....Bernard and Marie-Do....Hélène on the phone....Alphonse and Hélène walking....Marie-Do and Bernard....Hélène and Roland.... Alphonse and Bernard....Alphonse looking for a business in Boulogne.... Bernard and Françoise....Roland and Alphonse....Marie-Do and Bernard make love in his studio....Bernard works on a film....Alphonse alone.... The four at table....Marie-Do and Bernard in bed....Bernard alone.... Bernard meets Alphonse....Ernest searching for Alphonse....Hélène....

5-14. One of Bernard's projects is photographing interesting textures. Here, a tree stump

5–15. Marie-Do serves as an anchor in the film outside of memory. She is very much present, and she is the only one to make real plans for the future. She looks ahead, here

Bernard and Marie-Do....She explains she's leaving for Montevideo.... Hélène and Alphonse talking in a car....Roland gets in.

The film is an extraordinarily tight montage of images and sounds which are not primarily meant to advance the story line (although they do that too) but to describe a precise milieu, an aura. Compared with *Muriel* even *Hiroshima* and *Marienbad* had relatively linear plot structures. *Muriel* gives us a constantly challenging confrontation with memories and present events – a melange that closely approximates the structure of everyday experience in which memories, meaningful or not, constantly interpose themselves among events, meaningful or not. It is a brilliant structure which points directly ahead to the fragmentation of *Je t'aime, je t'aime*. But it is more than a technological feat: there very simply are no characters in the film without it.

The film concludes with a final meal – a party during which Bernard finally explodes. Françoise sets him off by daring to play with his tape recorder. He slaps her. Ernest finally discovers where Alphonse is staying and arrives just at the end of the meal. The avenging angel, he destroys not only Alphonse's contemporary fiction (he is, in fact, Alphonse's brother-in-law and his sister, Simone, is frantically looking for her husband) but also the fiction of his memory. Alphonse and Hélène have been arguing about a letter he says he sent her breaking a date. She never received it. Ernest never

5–16. 'Ne descends pas!' Robert gets it as if in a gangster film

posted the letter. Bernard films this climax to the *petit drâme*. Ernest sings a song, a nostalgic ballad about time and memory called 'Déjà'. Bernard leaves crying.

He goes to Robert's house and yells up at him: 'Descends! Non! Ne descends pas!' But it is too late. Robert comes out of the house and Bernard shoots him. Bernard prepares to leave town. Hélène goes searching for him at the house of some old friends in the old quarter of the city, where she finds some repose. Alphonse and Ernest prepare to leave. But Alphonse gives Ernest the slip and gets on a bus. Hélène goes to the railway station. She is told she is in the wrong place. The train for Paris now leaves from the *new* station.

The last image is a long shot of Hélène's apartment. Simone has arrived. She walks all through it looking for her husband. But it is too late. The film has ended some minutes before. We are left with a shot of the empty, disordered, white room.

The bits and pieces of the fractured lives of Hélène, Bernard, Alphonse and the others are organized into a glistening collage. The film has nearly one thousand cuts, according to Resnais: a complicated montage which is necessary in order to convey the density of the emotional lives of these people. *Muriel* is concretely a matter of comings and goings, small talk, dead time, quickly-eaten meals, aimless strolls, missed opportunities, compulsive

5–17. 'The centre of town, please.' 'Why, you're there!' The store is selling 'Hot Dogs'

entertainments, conversations with blunt ends, doors, open spaces, half-forgotten and mis-remembered pasts. It is more about forgetting than remembering, more about the lives people imagine that they lead rather than the ones they do.

No one in *Muriel* has such searing, weighty memories as its author (although Bernard thinks he does). What Alphonse and Hélène remember of World War II is mainly the insignificant details of their relationship, an affair that was over almost before it began, more important in the memory than in life. The framework of the film – Alphonse's visit after 25 years – allows Cayrol and Resnais to concentrate on this stew of imaginings. The rhythms of everyday life, which usually cover over the pain of memories and help us to mis-remember them, are broken by the visit. The characters, as Cayrol saw them,

are always between two memories, between two times, between two passions, unstable, badly put, not knowing the limits of their existence. . . .[1]

Resnais didn't like them, but

Jean Cayrol and I could not make them act differently – and I think we have to accept that.[2]

Hélène lives in a whitewashed apartment whose furniture she constantly sells out from underneath herself. 'You never know, when you wake up,'

5–18. Hélène pulls the curtain on a dinner party in the achingly white apartment. In a few minutes, the memory-plots of Alphonse, Bernard, and Hélène will be unveiled as well

Bernard says, 'if you'll be in the Second Empire or in Rustic Normandy.' 'Be careful of the china,' Hélène warns her dinner guests, 'it's very fragile porcelain, and it's been sold since yesterday.' Alphonse tells stories of his years in the north of Africa (which do not endear him to Bernard) but then his wife and brother-in-law show up at the end of the film. He has no apparent career, in fact, no existence outside of the limits of the film. Françoise is a cold woman. Her relationship with Alphonse never really makes dramatic sense – and that paradoxically makes it one of the touchstones of reality in the film. Roland de Smoke is as shadowy as his name. Bernard, much younger than the other major characters, is caught only for a while in their paralysis. But the action he takes, so unusual for a Resnais film, turns out to be based on bad faith. It isn't at all clear that Robert was uniquely responsible for the death of 'Muriel'. Suicide may have been a better course of action for Bernard. Anyway, Bernard hasn't the courage of his convictions: 'Descends! Non, ne descends pas!' The death is accidental.

Only the minor characters seem to have some sense of the 'limits of their lives'. Marie-Do is singularly attractive, self-possessed, and thoughtful, and Claudie – Hélène's best friend – may be flighty, but she lives her life in the present. Ernest's song – such an unusual break in the realistic action of this film – makes the point clearly:

You can be happy on this earth, but people don't know it, so they prefer to fear the future, bemoan the past, and say: 'Déjà'.

Muriel, ou le temps d'un retour is an anti-memory film.

We still haven't got to the point in Resnais's development at which we can identify with, admire, and respect the characters. (Whether or not it's important to do so is another question.) But we have arrived at a stage where they are recognizably human. The third level is reached in his next film, *La guerre est finie*, one of his most popular simply because its main characters are people one would like to know ..., well.

Much of this exhilaration one feels in watching *Muriel* is therefore not the result of the characters per se, and certainly not a function of the storyline, mundane as it is. It is, on the contrary, due to the masterful technique of the film. Our attention is still more attracted to the teller than the tale.

The language Resnais and Cayrol created for *Muriel* is possibly less immediately striking than the idiom of *Marienbad* but much more sophisticated, I think. There is still a sense that architectural materialism can communicate information about character, but the materialism of *Muriel* operates as symbol or objective correlative rather than crude simile. Cayrol picked Boulogne-sur-mer as the setting for the film with good reason. He explains:

5–19. Ernest sings 'Déjà'

I situated the story in Boulogne, despite Resnais's doubts, because Boulogne is also a town after a drama. There are two towns, the old one spared by the war and the reconstructed town, the topography of which the old inhabitants cannot recognize.[3]

Roland de Smoke is certain that Hélène's apartment is where his attic used to be. Townspeople argue about the former location of buildings as a pastime. In one quick, pointed scene in the middle of a film a man asked to be taken to the centre of town. 'Why, this is it!' comes the startled reply, reminiscent of Mephistopheles's reply to Faustus when he asks to be taken to hell: 'Why, this is hell, nor am I out of it!'

Multiple shots of new buildings and buildings under construction regularly punctuate *Muriel*. As the town plasters over the effects of the war, so do the characters. Both would be better off to recognize the memories, accept them, and integrate them into their personalities.

There are few if any tracking shots in *Muriel*, stylistically a radical departure for the master of the 'travelling'. Nor are there any flashbacks, equally remarkable considering Resnais's past reputation. (Nevertheless, Bernard's 8-mm home movie of Algeria certainly acts in the same way. But Bernard says it's 'evidence', not a memory.) *Muriel* is shot in an intense present tense; the past is words, words, words. Of all Resnais's films up to this point, it is the most realistic. Aside from one or two highly stylized performances (Delphine Seyrig's certainly, Kerien's and Thierrée's possibly) it has a documentary quality throughout. Although the interiors were shot on a set, Resnais had Jacques Saulnier, his art director, rebuild a real apartment he had seen in Boulogne precise down to the detail of the woodwork.

Perhaps the most striking attribute of *Muriel* is its colour cinematography. It is not only Resnais's first colour film but one of the most remarkable of the early sixties, a period in which filmmakers were discovering the realistic possibilities of newly improved colour filmstocks.

Many critics have commented on the colour quality of *Muriel*. Resnais and cinematographer Sacha Vierny have achieved a tone which is unusually luminous, limpid, and liquescent. This isn't at all easily seen in contemporary 16-mm prints (which is how most people must see *Muriel* these days) but should a new 35-mm print ever be struck from the original negative no doubt the fondly remembered colour of *Muriel* will be recaptured.

I asked Resnais how he achieved this. The answer was surprising:

In the simplest way. We decided with Sacha Vierny that we would stick with realist light, and that we would shoot the film exactly where the action would have taken place in Boulogne-sur-mer and we would not try to change the slightest thing for the colour. If it was raining, there would be rain. If there was sun there would be sun. We wouldn't pay any attention to that. Very simple.

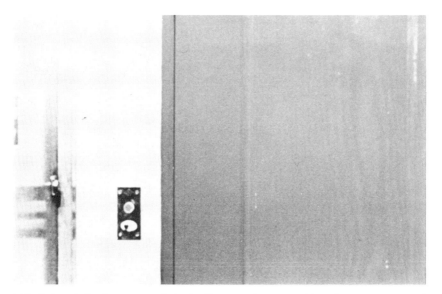

5-20. Before de Smoke enters, early in the film, Resnais gives us this striking composition of white wall, red door glistening in the overhead hall light, and doorbell button

'No special treatment for the filmstock?'

Absolutely not. No filters, nothing. Just complete simplicity. But it was in a way too because we had the feeling that in real life there are a lot of colours that we don't perceive and that in *Muriel* because of the editing (there are a lot of shots, nearly 1000) we would get some kind of effect. I wasn't sure what, but I had the feeling that the colour would become sometimes very aggressive, and so we just shot it.[4]

The effect is especially surprising to professionals because the walls in Hélène's apartment where much of the action takes place are pure white and it is very difficult indeed to shoot white on colour stock.

The montage of the film is less immediately obvious but equally impressive, on reflection. As we noted earlier, much of the montage was indicated in Cayrol's script. The basic concept of the film was clear from the beginning: a rugged, unadorned, realistic image overlaid with a touch of theatricality in the acting, the whole stitched together into a detailed mosaic which would best communicate both the tenor of everyday life for the characters and the febrile atmosphere in which they find themselves.

To this end, Cayrol suggested,

we can have a camera fairly independent of the story, turning around the intrigues, fleeing, then returning like a restless animal.[5]

It isn't strictly the camera that does this, but the image, through the

5–21. Resnais on the set of *Muriel*. Behind the lights 'outside' can be glimpsed the background of a photographed Boulogne

complicated montage. The image is a major 'actor' in the film. It replaces the narrator of *Marienbad* and therefore frees the characters. They are no longer prisoners of the narrator's persona.

It's interesting that we use two contrasting words for the job of putting together a film: editing (or cutting) and montage. The first suggests a reductive process, as if the job after shooting was to eliminate unwanted material. The second term, however, indicates a constructive project, building the final images of the film. For Resnais, the word is definitely montage. He shoots very little material that he doesn't eventually use.

In order to smooth over the many joints of *Muriel* he worked hard on the soundtrack (which is always the glue that holds the 'découpage' together). The soundtrack of *Muriel* has a life of its own. It, too, was carefully built up, not just to support the image track but to comment upon it and expand it. Much of the information we get about Boulogne comes to us almost subliminally from what we hear in the film. Antoine Bonfanti, perhaps the leading French sound technician of the New Wave period, did the recording for *Muriel*. The songs by the well-regarded avant-garde composer Hans Werner Henze are also used to heighten the reality of the image. Sung by Rita Streich, they had originally had lyrics that made specific comments on the milieu of the film. But Resnais felt this detracted from the significance of the images which accompanied them and intentionally adjusted them so that they were not so explicitly intelligible.

Some years later, Jean-Luc Godard would call for the liberation of the soundtrack from the 'tyranny' of the image track. Resnais foreshadowed him. He was also experimenting here with overlap cuts in which the sound of the previous image continues for a moment or two into the succeeding image. The effect is to weld the two together as no straight cut could. Within a few years, this became a commonplace of film syntax, observable in any television commercial and entirely accepted by viewers.

It was not the first time Resnais had introduced an innovation which later became a standard practice. In *Marienbad* he had developed a transition from a scene on one level of reality to a scene on another level which consisted of a rhythmic alternation of the two shots, with the periods of the previous shot gradually decreasing in length as the periods of the latter shot increased inversely. It's now commonly used for segues into dreams, fantasies, or memories.

But these are not simply technical innovations. In *Muriel*, technique and meaning coalesce. That's what makes the film the masterpiece it is. The camera and its image (and the sound recorder and its 'image') are central to the film. Bernard resurrects Muriel through film and tape and written diaries.

5–22. Bernard sees Hélène for the last time as she descends from his workroom where she has gone to look for him

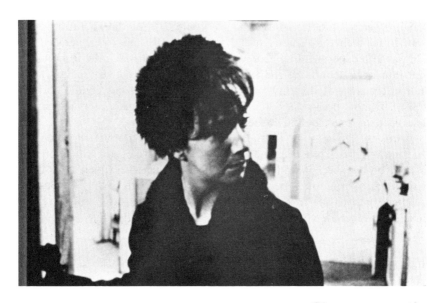

5–23. Simone comes looking for her husband, but the film is over...

5–24. ...and the room is entirely empty. The last shot.

Media are more than just tools in *Muriel*. He has captured the Algeria he imagines on scratchy, rough-grained, washed-out 8-mm film. Film is our collective memory: a terror for the people filmed, as well as the spectators, for they are caught, in the eternal moment, in frozen reality, condemned to live out their lives continually. This is the bad memory from which the characters in *Muriel* suffer.

For the first time in *Muriel* Resnais makes the oppression of imaged pasts human. In *Hiroshima*, it had been grandiose and awful; in *Marienbad*, abstract and intellectual; in *Muriel*, it is emotional and vital.

6. The Struggle Continues

Of all Alain Resnais's films, *La Guerre est finie* is the least tendentious, the most direct, and the most relevant. It is the only one of his films to date not only to use a contemporary setting, but also to deal with contemporary issues. It is Resnais's most accessible film and has reached a larger and more popular audience than any of the others. It deserves its reputation and following, certainly, but its apparent simplicity is deceptive.

It did not begin as an exercise in clarity. Originally, the screenplay was as complex in terms of montage as any of Resnais's earlier films. Gaston Bounoure, who stole a look at an early draft of Jorge Semprun's script against Resnais's wishes, reports that it included a far larger number of 'flashes' (flash-backs, flash-forwards, fantasies, imaginings) than eventually appear in the finished film. 'Reading it, one had the impression,' Bounoure writes, 'that these interior images constituted something like an entirely separate film, one that developed in the margins of the first.' Resnais apparently spent more time working on the script for *La Guerre est finie* than on any of his previous films, going through two entire early drafts, then changing a good deal during the shooting.

Why? In interviews, Resnais has always pointed towards the character of Diego Mora (Yves Montand) as the reason for the comparative simplicity of the narrative structure of the film. Since the character has clear motivations, the film must. But there are other reasons, as well. Resnais had not been satisfied with audience reaction to *Muriel*. He now thinks it might have been more effective to spend just a little more time establishing the relationships of the characters before plunging into the fragmented story. Because audiences tended to react against the initial confusion (rightly or wrongly) this coloured their experience of the film.

With *La Guerre est finie*, he was determined not to take audiences for granted. Unlike the earlier films – even *Hiroshima* – this film had something specific to say. It was imperative that style did not distort content, or divert attention from it. If anything, this attitude resulted in *La Guerre est finie* having a structure that was more sophisticated rather than less, if only because it was the subtle distillation of an earlier more elaborate and self-conscious scenario.

All New Wave directors shared this self-consciousness about style. It was inevitable. Not only had the majority of them come to filmmaking via critical analysis (no less Resnais, even if his criticism was the practical sort that takes place in an editing room), but their first efforts had been greeted with considerable praise because they seemed to be stylistically revolutionary. Of them all, only Jean-Luc Godard welcomed this public image. His aim, as he was to express it several years later, was to 'return to zero', to rewrite entirely the language of the cinema. Truffaut, like Resnais, retreated from early experimental freedom to a more cautious position. He felt that the limits of genre and convention were necessary elements of the productive dialectic of film. *La Guerre est finie* is hardly a genre film, but there is this same sense that it is more thoughtful, more mature if you will. It doesn't have to show off.

Resnais first approached Jorge Semprun with the suggestion that they make a film together in 1964. He had been drawn to him by reading Semprun's first novel, *Le Grand Voyage*, published in the early sixties: understandable since it was an uncanny evocation of so many of the themes Resnais himself had dealt with. (The hero has been deported from Spain after the Civil War and is on his way to Auschwitz. During the trip, he recollects his life in piecemeal fashion.) Interestingly, the film Resnais and Semprun eventually made contrasts with rather than extends this line of development.

According to Roy Armes, Resnais originally suggested two possible themes to Semprun: one dealt with the contemporary Greek situation (Semprun later wrote Costa-Gavras's landmark *Z*), the other with 'the efforts of a committee for peace in Vietnam or Algeria' (compare *Loin du Vietnam*). Either of these two subjects would have been more directly relevant (although the Colonels' putsch which gave *Z* such inherent drama was not to take place until 1967). But Semprun was of the opinion that the character of someone like Diego, a still-active Spanish militant twenty-five years after 'the war is over', would provide a broader base for the politics of the film. It also may have been closer to home for Semprun, who was born in Madrid in 1933.

Resnais's own aim, as he later stated it, was

to show that a professional revolutionary was a man who had the same banal concerns, day in and day out [as anyone else] and that at each moment of his life it was necessary that he make decisions. This was an excellent dramatic character because at all times he had before him choices that were important to make, whether they themselves were important or minuscule, because those choices might imperil his life or the survival of his organization. . . .[1]

Resnais had found a way to give urgency to the poetry of everyday life he had discovered in *Muriel*.

As a consequence, Diego is the first really likeable character in Resnais. The published script of the film is dedicated to Florence [Malraux] who had been part of his crew since the early fifties, had just been promoted to 'Assistant Director', and whom he was to marry in the late 1960s. It's not too much to assume that the character of Diego – and his relationship with Marianne – has a special attraction for Resnais. There's no identity of profession, but Diego certainly comes closer to the character of Resnais himself than anyone else in his films.

La Guerre est finie is, in fact, the first of Resnais's films in which a man is the central character. The films that follow *Muriel*, more assured, more active, less stylized, will all be seen from a male perspective. It is as if Bernard had won the aesthetic contest with his step-mother Hélène and established dominance in Resnais's filmic universe. When Bernard took action at the end of the film, he freed Resnais as well as himself. He is one of the very few younger characters in Resnais's films – nearly all Resnais's

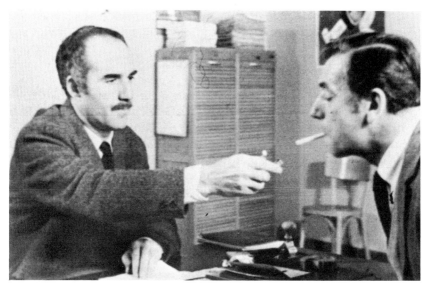

6–1. The same banal concerns. In the opening sequence of *La Guerre est finie*, professional cop Michel Piccoli lights professional revolutionary Yves Montand's cigarette during a rote interrogation

people are middle-aged (it being only at that point that they have accumulated sufficient past to be of interest) – and the note of youth that he introduced is continued in *La Guerre est finie.*

Diego's continual involvement in decision-making introduces an important new facet of Resnais's investigation into the phenomenon of imagination. In the past, alternate realities for Resnais's characters had been composed of equal parts memory and fantasy: both were essentially psychological. But now the life of the mind takes on new meaning: logical rather than emotional. The term 'flash-forward' which became common usage in describing the intervening imagery that is one of this film's more remarkable qualities is not really very precise. Diego doesn't summon up pictures of what is about to happen but rather alternatives of what might happen. At times they verge on daydreaming (as in his visualization of what Nadine Sallanches may look like – see pp. 100–1), at times they are strictly the products of an inquiring mind that must keep one step ahead of the enemy. In either case, they have a vitality that is new to Resnais. It's obvious that Diego and his colleagues are at least as obsessed with the past as any of Resnais's previous characters, but the tenor of the film is forward looking. For the first time in Resnais, the future is not only a consideration, but a pressing, imminent truth.

6–2. In the Sud-Express, going back to Paris once again, Diego lets his mind wander

6–3–6. Four possible images of Nadine Sallanches. In the dining car on the train Diego is over-hearing a nondescript gossipy conversation between a woman and her husband: 'If Lucienne left, believe me, it's not only to take care of the nephews. There's more to it than that.' 'You're always making mountains out of molehills.' 'If I mention it, it's because I have reason to know.... Can you imagine? Feeding that whole crowd, their husbands, and no Lucienne?!' The woman reminds Diego of his imaginary Nadine. He sees her descending a staircase, almost as if in the famous painting by Marcel Duchamp, and going out into the street. His four-faced Nadine is the result. He should trust his instincts. His first image of her is the truest.

6–7. 'Black coffee worldliness...' 'The likeable bum next to him in the cafe, it turns out, works for the cops'

Like *Muriel*, *La Guerre est finie* is divided into five sections, but this time instead of being acts in the classic dramatic structure, the sections are elements of a developing essay. The film has a circular structure. The first section, 'To Warn Juan' mirrors the last, 'To Warn Diego'. The film begins and ends with trips between France and Spain, but despite the circularity, there is an unavoidable sense of progression. The graph of the film is a section of a double helix.

Section 2, 'The Truths of the Lie' introduces the aging revolutionary context in which Diego must operate, then concentrates on the contrast between his continuing relationship with Marianne and his instant affair with Nadine. Section 3, 'Exile is a Tough Profession', develops the dichotomy between Diego's grizzled professionals and the new generation of amateur revolutionaries. This is the heart of *La Guerre est finie*. The penultimate section, 'A Slow, Stubborn Task of Edification which Goes on Indefinitely', resolves the conflict between the two political points of view (at least for Diego. The rest of us were to spend the decade arguing it!) The conclusion to the film suggests a new beginning. *La Guerre est finie* may seem to be a fairly loose narrative in the contemporary style, but its underpinnings rest on a tight, carefully worked-out structure of significance.

Diego Mora has been in exile so long that his French betrays no trace of an accent. (A subsidiary irony that Resnais must have appreciated is that he is played by an actor, who, in David Thomson's memorable phrases is able effortlessly to generate that particularly French 'spirit of black coffee worldliness', but was born in Italy.[2]) He has been living, in Paris, for a number of years with a Swedish woman, Marianne (Ingrid Thulin) who is as much an exile as he. For a quarter of a century, he has been a professional, resourceful political operative, his energies devoted wholly to overthrowing the Fascist regime in Spain. *La Guerre est finie* catches him at the moment in his life which has since come to be known as 'midlife crisis'. The continual round of underground journeys to and from his homeland, the perpetual calls for a general strike, the shopworn tactics, the rhetoric, the forms and postures, the ritualistic, repetitive actions – but not the goals – have begun to pall, just slightly. Yet he keeps on.

The film opens with his return to France after a long period in Spain. He has done this a hundred times before. This time he is stopped at the border. Yet it doesn't unnerve him. The patterns are so strongly established that he absolutely cannot believe that the police are on to him after so long and he even ignores a blatant clue. (The border guards know that he has been in Madrid.)

La Guerre est finie takes Diego from this entrance, Easter Sunday, 18 April 1965, 7:15 a.m., through three days in Paris, back to Spain again. On Wednesday morning, 21 April, at 11:30 a.m. Marianne leaves to follow him to Barcelona. It is now understood that it is he the police are searching for, not his compatriot Juan, as Diego thought at the beginning of the film. For the first time in all the years they have been together Marianne has a chance to join Diego in his work. The film ends.

During the course of his three days in Paris, Diego must confront two set of truths about himself: one concerning his work, the other his 'personal life'. (He has so little existence outside his work that the phrase is almost laughable when applied to Diego.) When asked the secret of life, the good doctor Freud once replied: 'Lieben und arbeiten.' Love and work. Diego's existence is reduced to these two essentials.

What makes *La Guerre est finie* one of the most important and vital films of the 1960s is that it is able to unify these twin concerns. The film is an elegant series of correspondences. Marianne is outside Diego's work, Nadine (Geneviève Bujold) is inside it. Diego's group looks to the long-term solution; Nadine's wants immediate gratification. A life with Marianne is probable; life with Nadine impossible. Love with Marianne comfortable; with Nadine exciting. It is not the little choices that present themselves to Diego daily (whether or not to enter a building, whether or not to smile at a policeman)

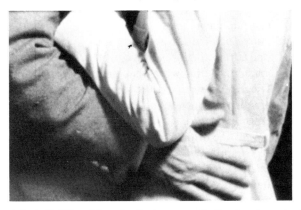

6–8. A–F. When Diego finally does meet Nadine (on the stairs, by the way) the outcome is almost preordained. A look, a touch, an embrace....

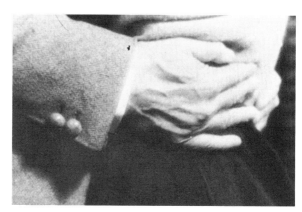

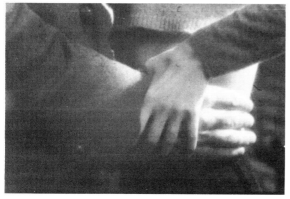

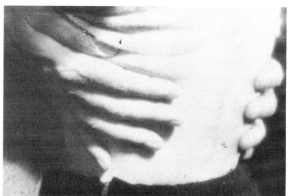

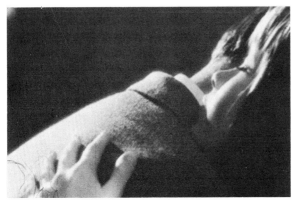

6–8. G–L. . . . They make love quickly, pleasantly, and rather unemotionally. Resnais breaks up Nadine into the parts of her body (legs, shoulders, feet). The emphasis is on the moment.

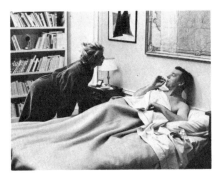

6–9. A–F. However, when Diego goes home to Marianne, the love scene that ensues is played – and shot – in direct contrast. It is slow, emotional, felt, and just a bit difficult. There is a past between these people. Marianne is always a whole woman, never seen in parts. And there is an aftermath that is just as important as the urgent sex.

that are ultimately significant, but these two big questions: to stay with the old way politically or to go with the new, and whether to choose Marianne or Nadine. The sum of those questions involves integrating love with work.

As Diego discovers, the questions answer themselves – they have already been answered by his life. He knows that the general strikes are futile and the rhetoric of his compatriots grey with age. He also knows that plastic explosives are futile, and the rhetoric of Nadine's companions purple, florid, and raw. He finally knows that neither choice is possible – and both are necessary. Politics is 'a slow, stubborn task of edification which goes on indefinitely'. He stays where he is, although it appears likely at the end of the film that he will realize that the time has come to try to build what seems equally futile – a personal life – with Marianne.

From this description of Diego's dilemma it may appear that *La Guerre est finie* is a pessimistic, even cynical film. Nothing could be further from the truth. Because Diego recognizes his situation he will be able to succeed. Antonio Gramsci had a phrase that could serve as a motto for the film. The pessimism of the intelligence, Gramsci said, is opposed by the 'optimism of the will'. An intelligent man, Diego nevertheless wills a future for himself.

6–10. When Diego arrives home after six months in Spain, Marianne and her colleagues are putting together the photographs of a book. It's an editing job, weaving together 'Bill's' 'real' photographs and the fantasy drawings of Folon and Topor. 'It's complicated to explain, but in pictures it's quite simple,' Marianne explains. It has to do with the language of cities, 'the way cities talk to people'. Not unlike the film.

6–11. Diego examines one of the photos. It seems to signify a right turn. 'Poor unhappy Spain. Heroic Spain. I've had enough of Spain: more than enough. Spain's become the lyrical rallying point of the entire left, a myth for veterans of past wars. . . . All Spain is anymore is a tourist's dream'.

Jorge Semprun chose not to focus on one of the specific political situations Resnais suggested, preferring instead to opt for a broader view of the political life. Although the film was popular when it was released that didn't necessarily prove anything about the sophistication of its politics, for it was, after all, quite an exciting modern love story. Yet with the benefit of hindsight we can see just how prescient *La Guerre est finie* actually was. First of all, it zeroed in immediately on what was probably the primary strategic argument among forces on the left during the late sixties and early seventies: whether or not to choose the 'soft' path (with all its general strikes, manifestoes, tactical retreats and endless disappointments) or the 'hard' – 'blow the bastards up'. In 1965 in the U.S., the political dialogue was still a couple of years away from a confrontation with this insoluble dilemma, although in France – where unlike the U.S. an intellectual political culture thrives – the lineaments of the battle were beginning to be seen.

Semprun not only identifies this crucial argument but comes up with what seems to me is the only valid solution to it. If the pessimism of the intelligence must coexist with the optimism of the will, it is also true that the 'hard' line which is the result of an emotional reaction to an unacceptable political situation must learn to express itself in terms of the 'soft' line which is the product of analysis.

6–12. Diego is infuriated when Nadine gives him a suitcase full of plastic explosives to hold without telling him what it is. He makes plans to meet her to tell her off. But the personal relationship between the two supersedes in the scene in the Métro.

6–13. The 'Revolutionary Action' group explains political matters to Diego. He is furious because he agrees with them, and because he also agrees with the people they disagree with.

Diego is not unmoved by the actions of Nadine and her colleagues. The young man who is the leader of the group sums up their argument for terrorism:

Tourism is one of the main sources of income for the regime. But there is another side to it: millions of people are getting used to the notion that Spain is a perfectly normal country. They tend to associate Spain with their vacation memories, which are necessarily pleasant. This is an extremely dangerous factor of political mystification, of demobilizing anti-Fascist action in Europe. We therefore have to strike a blow at tourism in Spain. Create a climate which will stop it, or at least slow it up....We obtain a double result: we stop the flow of foreign exchange, and we awaken the conscience of the masses.[3]

Diego can't let this last remark pass: 'You mean because it's asleep?' The 'Revolutionary Action' group's position is perfectly logical – too logical. It leaves no room for human error. More important, it assumes any political situation is soluble.

As it happened, in Spain, the end of the Franco regime came with a whimper, not a bang. Elsewhere in Europe, the victory of the left looks to be evolutionary rather than historically immediate. It is a slow, stubborn process of edification. The lesson of the sixties, both in the U.S. and Europe, was just this: that politics is not a matter of instant solutions, but rather a question of quirky, sometimes emotional, often illogical human reactions. If the masses don't want the revolution it's not a revolution.

There was a second important lesson in Semprun's broad survey of the political life. It, too, has proved its wisdom only with time. The love story of *La Guerre est finie* is not simply tacked on to the political story: it is a vital part of it. Diego must learn to live with Marianne. If anything really new ideologically came out of the ferment of the sixties it was the lesson of feminism that the revolution begins at home. Sexual politics is the microcosm which faithfully reflects national politics. This line isn't as clearly stated in the film as the question of tactics and strategy in Spain, but it pervades the mood of the film. If it isn't explicit, that's only because there were few available social models at the time for Semprun and Resnais to use dramatically.

These twin insights of *La Guerre est finie* are foreshadowed in the quotation from Sartre which is used as an epigraph for the published version of the script. It describes the thrust of the film so clearly that it is worth quoting in full:

The militant does not ask that his action justify him: he *is*, and needs no subsequent justification. But his personality encompasses his own justification, since it is constituted by the end to be attained. Thus it is relative to the action, which itself is

6–14. Diego's revolution isn't very colourful. More a matter of empty urban vistas, slow, stubborn suburbs

relative to the goal. As for the action itself, it should rightly be termed an undertaking, for it is a slow, stubborn task of edification, which goes on indefinitely.

The prose may be a bit over-fine, but the film makes these ideas concrete. Sartre unites politics with personality, and this after all became one of the main underpinnings of radical politics in the seventies: the close identification between the way a life is lived and the specific political goals that are set. *La Guerre est finie* integrates the everyday details of Diego's life with the political form of it. Factually, he must confront during the film the poignant stretches of time that reach out behind him – that wealth of experience to which the title of the film ironically refers. That he does so, that he understands the regressive pressure of the past – and that he still returns again to Spain at the end of the film, are acts of moral and political courage and sanity which the younger people within the film (and outside of it) may not have understood at the time.

But now that their war too is over, the film takes on a different function: it is a shared experience now, not a portrait of differences. We now understand better that the political life is an organic whole, which grows and changes and is never complete, never perfect: revolution is a process, not an end.

Nothing in the *mise en scène* of Renais's previous films quite prepares one for *La Guerre est finie*. Because this film had so much to say that was specific and relevant, Resnais, working with Semprun, devised a voice for it that was quite different from *Muriel*, *Marienbad*, and *Hiroshima*.

The first concern was timeliness. Resnais has often spoken of his perception of the difficulty of making a film precisely contemporaneous. As he expressed it in an interview in 1962:

It's very difficult from the moment you accept making a fiction film with characters who express themselves through everyday language, it's difficult to make them speak properly in an everyday manner about immediate things.... The length of time between the moment of writing and the release of the completed film would have to be no more than a month, or a month and a half.[4]

He exaggerates, but only slightly. *La Guerre est finie* was geared precisely to a specific time, only a few months before the actual shooting. The strike which takes place on 30 April in the film, for example, was real, as were the manifestoes. To increase the chances of obtaining 'everyday language' in the film, Resnais avoided the theatrical actors he had preferred for his earlier films and assembled a cast composed entirely of film actors and unknowns. The result is a more muted tone, a lack of distancing, and a sharper verisimilitude. Ingrid Thulin, interestingly enough, is not unlike Delphine Seyrig in looks, movement, and gesture. But she is gutsier, more direct, less affected.

The music for the film, too, was designed to be naturalistic, conversational, and less intrusive. In the earlier films, Giovanni Fusco, Francis Seyrig, and Hans Werner Henze had provided sharply modernist accompaniments which worked against the grain of the image, strengthening it by contrast. Now Fusco has composed a score which is notable for its selflessness. Likewise, the photography by Sacha Vierny is in the soft, realist style he used for the French sequences of *Hiroshima*, but with a touch of tonal exaggeration.

The cinematic idiom of *La Guerre est finie* is interesting, but nowhere near as important as it was earlier for Resnais, when it was often if not always one of the main subjects of the film. This film isn't a matter of style, it's a matter of Diego. There's a touch of Bogart here, and that undoubtedly accounted for some of the popularity of the film. It is, after all, possible to see it as a love story without bothering oneself about ideology and strategy. But Yves Montand has always put that 'black coffee worldliness' in the service of other, more ambitious aims than romantic sentimentalism.

Like his predecessors in Resnais's cinematic universe. Diego has trouble with names. He is, variously, known as Domingo, Carlos, Diego, and Gabriel Chauvin. But where as He, She, A, X, and the others were circumscribed by

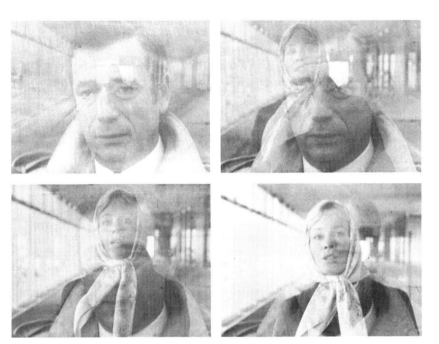

6–15. A–D. In the focal sequence of the film, a dissolve, Marianne's and Diego's images of each other slowly merge together

namelessness, Diego is multiplied by his aliases. He welcomes the variety. It's useful. As he is about to leave for Spain again at the end of the film Diego jokes with his driver:

DIEGO: Shall we tell each other the story of our lives once we get started?
THE MAN: The real story or the false?
They laugh.
DEIGO: I'll tell the false. The real one is of no importance.

There's an echo here of the obsessions of the earlier films, but the tone contrasts significantly. Unlike the earlier characters, Diego is comfortable with the multiplicity of his memories. He is at peace with himself. He is Resnais's first well-integrated character and as such he looms a little larger than life: the deaths, the mistakes, the air of tired futility which provide the background to the film's politics are transcended: 'The militant does not ask that his actions justify him: he *is* and needs no subsequent justification.'

That is why *La Guerre est finie* is – and must be – a love story. A few years later Godard dreamed up a couple of lovers who were for him the true revolutionaries. Why? Because they 'made love, conversation, and progress. All at the same time'. Diego's private life with Marianne, so separate from his politics at the beginning ('I even began to wonder whether you really existed,' says Agnès, a friend of Marianne's when she meets him for the first time) converges with it at the end. The interior dialogue that the narrator (Jorge Semprun himself) has been holding with Diego stops. We pull back from Diego's point of view which has dominated the film from the beginning, and shift to Marianne's. She becomes the active character finally as she flies to Spain to warn Diego. The images of the two of them alternate and merge. A unity has been achieved.

Diego and Marianne. Diego and his past. Diego and his future. John Ward, in his useful book *Alain Resnais, or the Theme of Time*, very well expresses in a broader context this process of integration:

... 'this plunge into ourselves', our memories, and our pasts, will teach us that we are free and enable us to rediscover our capacity for action and the community between ourselves and others.[5]

For Alain Resnais in *La Guerre est finie* for the first time the dialectic with memory *does* work this way.

La guerre est finie, perhaps, but to borrow a phrase from the near-revolution of 68: la lutte continue!

In direct contrast to Diego is the 'Claude Ridder' of Resnais's segment of *Loin du Vietnam (Far From Vietnam)*. Old friend Chris Marker had the idea to put together this cinematic essay on the Vietnam question. As it turned out, the film is mainly about the impossibility of making a film about Vietnam from and in France.

William Klein contributed an affecting interview with the widow of Norman Morrison, the Quaker who became the first American to immolate himself in protest against the U.S. intervention in Vietnam. Klein also shot interviews with other Americans which have interesting documentary value. Joris Ivens contributed documentary footage from Vietnam which gives an interesting sense of how the people coped with the bombings which were in their own insouciant way the equal of the horror of *Hiroshima*. Even by 1967 it was clear that the United States was intent on destroying the country absolutely rather than admitting error. Claude Lelouch contributed some romantic footage of the U.S. Air Force which was more than pointless in terms of the film.

It was the segments directed by Resnais and Godard, however, that give the film perspective. Godard's consists mainly of a long take of Godard himself standing next to a Mitchell camera sporting antennae-like spotlights.

He explains why it is impossible for him to make the film he wants to make. The North Vietnamese won't let him into their country, and rightly so, he thinks, for why should they trust him, a French intellectual, to present their truth? Anyway, he concludes, the real film about Vietnam should be made by Vietnamese.

Like Godard, Resnais has constructed a monologue which strictly adheres to the theme of the film: what can French intellectuals and filmmakers do about the terror in Vietnam when they are so far removed from it? How responsible are they for it? Resnais's segment is the only fictional element in the film. Jacques Sternberg wrote the piece, using the character of 'Claude Ridder' on loan from *Je t'aime, je t'aime* (but luckily for *Je t'aime*'s Claude Ridder, played by a different actor, Bernard Fresson, who had first worked for Resnais in *Hiroshima* and was Diego's driver at the end of *La Guerre es finie*.) He serves as the symbol of bad faith in the film.

Whereas Godard's soliloquy presents a depressing but understandable alternative of paralysis in the face of the war, Resnais's concentrates on unacceptable inaction. It is, in attitude, 180 degrees opposed to Godard's. For Godard, action is impossible because of the distance, both metaphorically

6–16. 'Claude Ridder' (Bernard Fresson) begins his apologia for inaction

and literally. It is a practical analysis. For Ridder, action is a choice: one which he has decided not to make. The two episodes taken together provide the kernel of the moral problem posed in *Loin du Vietnam*: Resnais's the negative aspect, Godard's more positive. Although he probably did not know it at the time, Godard was going to spend much of the next five years trying to deal with this question: how can a filmmaker take part in political struggles which essentially are the concern of other people? How can the passive intellectual have an active effect?

This is the impetus behind Resnais's episode as well, but Resnais takes a more jaundiced view of it. 'Claude Ridder' is a leftist intellectual who has an assignment to review Herman Kahn's masterpiece of Strangelovian logic, *On Escalation*. In his monologue, explaining why he can't write the review, he pours forth his guilt about Vietnam, and vacillates to an inconclusive conclusion. He decides not to decide.

As political man, Ridder is the precise opposite of Diego. Where Diego is active, Ridder is passive. Where Diego and Marianne evolve a mutual, balanced relationship, Ridder and his woman are isolated from each other: she appears to exist only to listen to him talk. If Diego impresses with his authenticity, Ridder impresses with his inauthenticity.

6–17. Karen Blanguernon, (his unnamed and unspeaking girlfriend, listens)

6–18. At his desk, Ridder, flanked by an Antiballistic-missile model, carefully arranges his papers. But the light is glaring

Resnais's and Godard's episodes, although apparently not planned as such, nevertheless work closely together within the context of *Loin du Vietnam*. They are the only two episodes in the film that come to grips with the central question: what is one to do? For Godard, the subject is clear: himself, his own attitudes, his own ineffectuality. For Resnais, a parallel commentary must be phrased in fictional terms. The leverage of fiction is a necessity. In Resnais's episode, the listener is inside the frame, in Godard's outside it. By letting us see the listener, Resnais draws our attention to the moral question involved in observation. At least from a distance, that was what Vietnam was all about.

Although it comes into play only tangentially in Resnais's episode from *Loin du Vietnam*, his own attitude towards the political utility of cinema includes reservations. Even though Resnais has had a reputation since at least 'Guernica' and 'Nuit et Brouillard' as a 'political' filmmaker, the ideology of his films has never been elaborate. There is seldom a clear political message. 'I think maybe you can try to have that in a documentary,' Resnais explains, 'but if you deal with fiction, it's very difficult, because if you have some respect for character, the character very often takes over.'

I have nothing against very politically oriented pictures but I think it has to come from the script. But at the same time, when you are not shooting a documentary, I am slightly sceptical. . . .I think, you have TV, you have newspapers, you have books, and sometimes when you feel that the thing you have to say would be more effective in a book or a newspaper, you have to admit it.[6]

It's an interesting analysis of the problem of political film, and goes a long way to explaining the difference between Godard's hesitations in *Loin du Vietnam*, those of a filmmaker, and Claude Ridder's, those of a writer. In a sense, Ridder has a significantly greater moral responsibility simply because of his chosen medium.

7. La Vie de Montage

For anyone with even the mildest interest in the particular cinematic concerns of Alain Resnais, *Je t'aime, je t'aime* should be thoroughly irresistible. It's not so fully realized a film as *La Guerre est finie*, nor is it as assured as *Stavisky...*, but of all Resnais's films to date it is the quintessential distillation of his obsession with time, memory, and the imagination. Sadly, *Je t'aime, je t'aime* has been the least successful of Resnais's efforts commercially. Partly, this was due to bad timing. The film was shot in the Autumn of 1967 and premiered in Paris at the end of April 1968. The 'events of May-June', as they are

7–1. The Rug Dream: Friday, 1 November 1963. Evening.

now circumspectly known, were just building to a climax at that time and *Je t'aime*, despite some excellent reviews, got lost in the shuffle. English-speaking audiences did not see the film until four years later. (It was shown at the New York Film Festival in 1970, and released in the U.S. two years later.) If French audiences were confused by the unique and startling shape of *Je t'aime, je t'aime*, they at least had the advantage of understanding the dense dialogue. English speaking audiences, for the most part forced to rely on subtitles which couldn't hope to reproduce the poetry and subtlety of the soundtrack of the film, were at a total loss.

At least partially, *Je t'aime, je t'aime*'s poor reception at the box office was responsible for Resnais's forced absence from the screen for more than five years. Of all his films, however, it best repays repeated viewings. Indeed, viewers who extend themselves a little eventually become addicted to *Je t'aime*. Even now the film is so little known that it cannot even be said to have a cult reputation, but it is such a novel and exhilarating experience that it is to be hoped that this state of affairs will soon change.

What is attractive about *Je t'aime* is its beautifully simple thesis. It is an editor's film par excellence. It gives us a portrait of one Claude Ridder, who has worked in publishing, lived with a woman named Catrine, and attempted suicide after her death. The story is less complex than any in Resnais, but the telling of it – achronologically – is exuberant and masterful. Asked what the 'plot' of *Je t'aime, je t'aime* was, Resnais replied cryptically: 'A man meets a woman. That's all.' The découpage of the film, which seems complex at first viewing, is actually among the simplest in Resnais. The film has only about 334 shots (as opposed to almost a thousand in *Muriel*). The problem for audiences is that the bits and pieces of Claude Ridder's life are given to us in no particular chronological order.

In a way, this is Resnais's most practical, least theoretical film. It's provenance lies in his experience in the 1950s as a film editor. Anyone who has had the experience of discovering the power of the editing table to analyse the rhythms and mysteries of reality will understand Resnais's premise immediately. The aim of *Je t'aime, je t'aime*, it seems to me, is simply to share that experience with audiences.

All theories of film art, in one way or another, eventually trace their roots to two interrelated but apposite attributes of the medium. On the one hand, film comes as close as any technological device yet invented to capturing reality whole. On the other, just because it is so thoroughly mimetic, film can shape, change, or distort reality, or reveal qualities about it that we never before knew existed. As a scientific tool, film is used both ways. Anthropologists use it to capture reality; physicists, biologists, and naturalists use it to distort reality in useful ways.

7–2–4. Ridder's women. 2. With Catrine (Olga Georges-Picot) in the Glasgow hotel room. Thursday, 4 January 1967. 7:30 p.m. 3. With Wiana (Anouk Ferjac) at her place in Paris.

4. Marie-Noire (Marie-Blanche Vergne) waits for him in the hallway, Sunday, 2 January 1966, 12:30 a.m.

Time passing ?

7–5. 'Flashback.' Another hospital corridor. This time Institut Crespel, Thursday, 31 August 1967, 12:30 p.m.

Film theories that focus on the power of film to capture and preserve the real world are generally termed 'realist', while those theories that find the shaping, distortive power of film most interesting are usually grouped under the heading of 'expressionist'. Until the 1950s and 1960s, realism was almost always associated with mise en scène and expressionism with montage. One of the most important critical contributions of André Bazin and his colleagues on *Cahiers du Cinéma* (especially Godard) was to re-examine this old dichotomy and redefine realism with more sophistication. Bazin's suggested a realism that was more moral than technical and Godard, in several of his essays, explained how montage and mise en scène worked together in such a way that it was specious to classify types of cinema according to their relationship to either one or the other. What Bazin and Godard were working out in theory in the fifties, Resnais was learning in practice. He uses film as an investigative tool, and he is always sharply conscious of his relationship – through film – to audiences, so that despite the prevalence in his work of dreams, fantasies, and surrealist touches (which always used to be signs of antirealism) he is, in Bazin's sense, clearly a realist – of the moral sort. He has also understood better than any other contemporary director, just how the

7–6. The montage of *mise en scène*. Ridder finds himself wedged between two Nicoles in Wiana's bathroom. Wednesday, 5 March 1963, 10 a.m. 'Which one do you choose? The one on the left, or the one on the right?' 'The one on the left.' 'Ah! What a bad choice!'

7–7. Jacques Sternberg and Resnais during the shooting of *Je t'aime, je t'aime*. Tuesday, 5 September 1967, 4 p.m.

tool of montage can be used to reveal reality rather than to distort it. We are talking about the reality of imagination, of course, not the reality of materialism, yet even in this latter area, Resnais's technique works. See *Marienbad*, or *Muriel*.

Je t'aime, je t'aime is, quite simply, Resnais's masterpiece of realistic montage. Audiences may be put off initially, but once they learn the new idiom it becomes evident that the fictional character of Claude Ridder comes across clearer and sharper by several magnitudes simply because it is not encased in a conventional narrative. *Je t'aime* has the revelatory force of a hyper-realist portrait. Or a dream. And Ridder, despite the fact that he is a notably dull character (and not especially admirable) stays in the mind with a clarity unmatched by characters in more traditional narratives. In a sense, this is a sort of cubist approach to film. The perceived narration is broken down into elements which are rearranged according to a different, and it is to be hoped, more revealing logic.

Resnais first approached Jacques Sternberg, the novelist, with the idea of doing a film in 1962. Sternberg says he then gave Resnais notes for six possible projects, 'of which four were very bad and one I liked a lot'.[1] After Resnais had chosen, Sternberg turned out a sixty-page treatment for the film. Then the long process of gestation began. Over a period of three or four years he developed an enormous amount of material: bits and pieces of Claude Ridder's life, with dialogue, ranging over 15 years. By the time the material (one can hardly call it a screenplay) for *Je t'aime, je t'aime* had reached the point of critical mass, Resnais was busy with *La Guerre est finie*. The project lay fallow for still another two years before it was finally shot in late 1967.

The film bears some evidence of this five-year process. It is not, first of all, what we should have expected from Resnais after the politics and rather conventional narrative of *La Guerre est finie*. It is, in fact, a lot closer to *Marienbad*, the film Resnais had just shot before the project was conceived. Moreover, the lengthy period of gestation was a structural necessity. Sternberg worked slowly. He was intent on developing a story nonchronologically and this, as it happened, took a lot longer than simply writing 'Once upon a time, ... and then, ... and then'.

Eventually he resorted to a kind of 'automatic writing'. He turned out between five and eight hundred pages of script – a 'mountain' of potential material, most of it scenes which lasted a couple of minutes or less. Resnais, in the end, edited this material, choosing the *trenches de vie* which appear in the final shooting script. Throughout this, the process of editing – of distillation – was crucial. Resnais had Sternberg produce lengthy dossiers on each of the major characters. It was necessary to know them completely before choosing the moments of their lives that would be apotheosized in film. More than four fifths of the 'story' of Claude Ridder remains unshot. It's interesting to speculate whether this structure would work for a television serial. The two forms are not dissimilar. The idea of a serial is not to tell a straight story but to 'expose' a character to an audience through a long series of incidents. The structure of the total plot is relatively unimportant. (In American series, characters seldom grow or change, and the series ends in midstory when the contract is not renewed. In 'serials', however, the ideas of beginning, middle, and end have some validity.) What counts is the time spent with the people. As a boy, Resnais was fascinated by the serials of Louis Feuillade. It would be nice if he had the opportunity one day to try his hand at the form.

As an editor, Resnais understood that the essence of film montage is to 'approach the condition of music'. Musical terms like rhythm, harmony, counterpoint, and dissonance come into play. In abstract film, this aspect governs the entire work. *Je t'aime* comes as close as any straight narrative film to capturing the harmonic and rhythmic qualities of the medium. Although the sum effect of this quasi-musical structure is felt at first viewing, an understanding of how the various elements work together must wait for

7–8. Ridder in his study, Saturday, 5 August 1967, listening to Thelonius Monk

more detailed analysis. Resnais and Sternberg had to tread a fine line between being too abstruse and being too mundane. A haphazard selection of scenes from Ridder's life would have fallen flat, yet too much information, too many repetitions, would conversely have destroyed the necessary mystery of the film, for Claude Ridder is intentionally a relatively uninteresting character.

Je t'aime, je t'aime – the doubling of the title mirrors the doubling of times and sentiments within the film – *Je t'aime, je t'aime* is a glistening mosaic. Resnais fits it into a framework of science fiction which allows him a rational reason to break the life of Claude Ridder into pieces and rearrange them according to a higher logic than chronology.

Let me straighten out the history of Claude Ridder as we eventually come to know it. Ridder apparently served in the Resistance during the war (this is the closest we ever get to politics in the film). In the early fifties he got a job working in the warehouse of a publishing company. Gradually over the years he seems to have moved into a desk job, first dealing with the business end of publishing, later somewhat more involved in the editorial process. He is, throughout, an alienated modern man, and not even an especially attractive one. On 9 June 1959, a young woman named Catrine came to work at Ridder's firm. He was first introduced to her about one o'clock in the afternoon that day. The relationship developed rapidly.

7–9. The last ten seconds in Ridder's life before he meets Catrine, who is just entering behind him. Tuesday, 9 June 1959, 1 p.m.

Over the next seven and a half years Ridder and Catrine lived together spasmodically. The relationship was not a smooth one. Catrine eventually proved to be even more alienated than Claude, at times suicidal. They seem to have spent a lot of time together on vacations; even more time in the various apartments they shared (although the evidence we have regarding Ridder's interest and pastimes is distorted by the shape of the film, as we shall see). Ridder also spent considerable time with a woman who is apparently an old friend of his, Wiana Lust. Occasionally, he met another old friend, Bernard Hannecart, and his wife Marcelle. At one point in the mid-sixties, Ridder developed a connection with a young girl named Marie-Noire Demoor, even more neurotic than Catrine. It appears that Ridder lives in Brussels.

On 24 September 1962 at four o'clock in the afternoon Ridder, who was spending the day at a northern beach, noticed something very strange: a small white mouse ran across the empty sand. Late in the evening of 1 November of the following year Ridder had a dream in which he found himself squeezed between a wall and an oriental rug. On 5 March 1963, he had gone to visit Wiana, only to find that she was not at home. An attractive young woman named Nicole was about to have a bath in Wiana's flat. She asked him to wash her back, which he did. He did not make love to her. He did not see her again. But the memory stayed with him. On 5 September 1966

7–10. Monday, 24 September 1962. 'What the...!' Ridder notices the white mouse on the beach. He will not know the source of this phenomenon until almost five years later. The mouse has escaped from the time sphere. This is the only instance of 'doubling' interference between present and past in the film.

Ridder and Catrine were on vacation on the Riviera. At 4 p.m. that afternoon Ridder went snorkling while Catrine stayed on the beach. The weather was warm, the beach deserted. Ridder saw two sea serpents, several sharks, and some giant jellyfish during his short, but pleasant expedition [*Was it nice? Very. Did you see a lot of fish?*]

Early in January 1967, Ridder and Catrine visited Glasgow. On the evening of the fourth of January, Ridder went out, leaving Catrine alone in the hotel room. When he returned, she was dead. Asphyxiated by gas escaping from the heater. With Catrine gone, Ridder sank into a true depression. On 4, 5, and 6 March 1967, he seems to have spent a lot of time with Wiana, talking about Catrine's death. He felt morally responsible. On the fifth of August that year, alone in his apartment, Ridder put on a record of Thelonius Monk's 'Misterioso'. After a while, he sat down on the floor with his back against the bed. Almost on impulse, he put a revolver to his chest and pulled the trigger. Ridder spent most of the month of August recuperating in hospital.

When he was released from the hospital on Thursday, 31 August 1967, he was met by two men from the Crespel laboratories, not far away. They asked him to come with them. 'Why not?' he replied. They asked him if he would be willing to participate in an experiment. They had built a time machine.

7–11–13. The framework of *Je t'aime, je t'aime*. 11. Ridder approached by Moyens and Rhuys, the scientists, after being released from hospital, Thursday, 31 August 1967, 10.30 a.m. 12. The laboratory, Tuesday, 5 September 1967 shortly after 4 p.m. The machine is at rear, a drole construction which is part brain, part organic flying saucer, with 'pins' stuck in it. The set has a refreshing lack of pretension. 13. In the sphere, during one of their moments in the present. Ridder and his travelling companion.

It worked with mice, but would it work with humans? They didn't know. Ridder had already attempted suicide. His will to live was none too strong, even now. Little would be lost if the experiment didn't work. He agreed.

On 5 September 1967, at precisely 4 p.m. Ridder entered the machine, and travelled back one year to the episode on the beach. He saw himself entering the water, swimming, leaving the water, not necessarily in that order. [*Was it nice?*] The experiment is supposed to last one minute, but something goes wrong. Ridder is stuck in the machine. He relives the moments of his life recounted above (and others), sometimes repeatedly. When he reaches the moment of attempted suicide he is thrown free. He dies on the lawn of the Crespel Institute.

Or maybe he doesn't. In any event, as the head of the institute says in the last words of the film:

We'll have to redo all our calculations[2]

But Resnais's calculations are nearly perfect. After five years and 800 pages of screenplay, he and Jacques Sternberg have distilled the irreducible essence of Claude Ridder's short unhappy life, such as it is. It explodes on the screen.

I haven't covered all the episodes of Ridder's past to which we are exposed – far from it: nearly a hundred separate scenes of varying lengths are visited and revisited during Ridder's abortive trip. And of course, to 'chronologize'

7–14. The focal point of *Je t'aime, je t'aime*: snorkling in the Mediterranean precisely a year before the trip begins. Monday 5 September 1966. Compare 7–18, p. 135. Ridder floats in space as well as time. Maybe that's why the experiment fails.

7–15. Le temp mort. Shortly after the shot in 7–9 (p. 129), this shot. Ridder's ritual

these episodes is to rob them of some of their significance. It is clear that Ridder returns to scenes that have some meaning for him. Many of them have to do with vacations (since the target period happened also to be within the time span of his vacation a year earlier). The majority have to do with Catrine, both because he spent most of the last seven years with her and because she was the principal emotional fact in his rather cool existence. A good number, however, seem inexplicable, although repeating viewings of the film and close study would no doubt reveal their significance.

Seventeen of the 95 episodes which add up to the life of Claude Ridder are significant enough to be visited repeatedly (some as many as six times). The beach scene on 5 September 1966 is used repeatedly as a punctuation mark, doubled and redoubled, sometimes barely a second, other times the full scene. [*Was it nice? Very. Did you see a lot of fish?*] The majority of the scenes have either to do with Ridder's work or his life with Catrine, or with the other three women with whom he seems to have been involved during this period. Some (like the quick shot of Claude squeezing between a wall and a rug) are fairly evident dreams. A good number have to do with *temps morts*: waiting for a tram, sitting on a beach, listening to music, eating. Sternberg and Resnais have been careful not to limit themselves in conventional dramatic fashion only to those moments which have 'significance' to Ridder's story. 'When you go back into the past in cinema,' Sternberg explained, 'it is almost always to participate in important, privileged scenes.

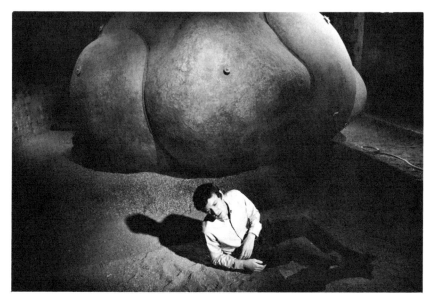

7–16. This time around, Ridder dies slowly, and in many places. His basic pose in the film has been this stretched out posture, usually lying on a bed or a beach with Catrine.

7–17. Tuesday, 6 September 1967, 6 p.m. The technicians finally find him on the lawn outside the sphere room. 'We'll have to redo all the calculations'

It is as if you were on the psychoanalyst's couch. I wanted, on the contrary, to choose totally insignificant scenes, *temps morts.*'[3] [*Was it nice? Very.*]

The summary above gives some sense of this rhythmic mosaic but the total effect of the film can't be conveyed in words. Each scene has been pruned to a precise length to relate to the ones that come before it and after it structurally rather than in terms of plot, and the result is mesmeric. This is as close to the condition of dreaming and unconsciousness as we can come in cinema, and it is also surprisingly exhilarating. We know, watching the film, that one of the primary psychological desires associated with cinema is the wish to freeze the past. *Je t'aime, je t'aime* fulfils the long-ago promise of Keats's Grecian Urn. For an hour and a half, Claude Ridder's rather mundane existence becomes more important than our own, not as a story as in most good fiction films, but in toto, almost in spite of its story: for its tram-waiting moments, for its swimming moments, for its sleeping moments, for its dead times as well as its drama.

It must be remembered that none of the scenes of the film are identified according to place and time (the details in the summary above come from the published version of the script), nor are they presented in any particular order, although Resnais does make a few concessions to dramatic chronological logic, for instance allowing Ridder's introduction to Catrine to come

7–18. Ridder is leaving the water here (see 7–14, p. 132), but walking backwards because of his flippers! An omen of things to come precisely a year later. 'Was it nice?'

early in the series. Whatever effect the life of Ridder has on us must come not from an imposed dramatic structure – there is none – but from its substance.

It may be useful to categorize the 334 shots into which *Je t'aime, je t'aime* is divided. The chart on pp. 138–9 lists all of the 'flashbacks' with their frequencies. The film begins, by the way, in late August 1967, with Ridder recuperating in the hospital. It ends with his apparent death on the lawn. Here are the categories: One hundred and fifty-one shots out of 334 consist of 'flashbacks' (although Resnais doesn't like that word in this context; 'I have the impression', he said, 'that this is a kind of eternal present. The hero revisits his past, but when he does, we are always with him. The film unreels, I think, always in the present. There is absolutely nothing like a flashback.'[4] The remainder are divided between the narrative before the time trip begins and brief punctuational returns to the machine during the trip.

Several basic focal points can be identified within the trip. These are listed here together with the number of shots devoted to each:

- On the beach on the Riviera exactly a year earlier (20)
- With Catrine on trains, on other beaches, at home (at least two different apartments at different times), in the streets of Brussels, et cetera (42)
- At his job: stock room, advertising, magazines, offices (18)
- In a gorge in Provence (3)
- With Nicole (1)
- With various friends (9)
- Miscellaneous: on a tram, in a street, et cetera (*temps morts*) (21)
- With Wiana (13)
- In the hospital (flashbacks only) (3)
- With the Glasgow police after Catrine's death (3)
- In the hotel room in Glasgow (10)
- Flashbacks to the Institut Crespel (10)
- In his apartment about to attempt suicide (3)

As the chart clearly shows, the moments of the film are far from arbitrary. That would most definitely be boring. Ridder and Resnais have chosen scenes that do have meaning, but not in the usual dramatic sense. This is a drama outside time. There is no pattern of development, recognition, peripeteia, and catharsis. Rather, like most of our lives – at least as we are capable of remembering them – it consists of model psychological scenes which we return to again and again whether or not they seem on the surface to have dramatic significance. *Je t'aime, je t'aime* is the perfect subconscious diary.

Perhaps the most haunting moment of the film is the single one which is not chosen in some way, logical or illogical, but which is forced upon Ridder by

7–19-21. Ridder stretched out in life and, in the other direction, in death

Alain Resnais

The Scenes of *Je t'aime, je t'aime*

1951	1952	1953
7 December 11:00		5 January 15:00
		24 December
		(evening)

1957	1958	1959
		9 June 13:00[1] (2)
		9 June 18:00 (2)
		10 June 21:00
		13 September 15:00
		20 October 12:00
		26 October 10:00
		5 December 10:00
		7 December 12:00

1963	1964	1965
1 February 4:00	7 March 18:00	1 April 1:00
3 February 12:00	5 September 13:30 (2)	22 April 1:00 (2)
6 February 20:00 (2)	5 September 17:00	3 May 10:30
5 March 10:00[3]	15 September 17:00	17 May 22:00
7 March 17:00	22 September 13:00	18 May 21:30
27 June 16:00	11 October (night)	26 May 22:00
13 October 21:00	11 October 6:00	5 June 13:00
1 November (evening)[4]	13 October 22:00 (2)	1 September 20:00 (2)
2 November 22:00	16 October 5:00	5 October 12:00
5 November 16:00		
23 November 24:00		

[1] First meeting with Catrine   [2] The mouse on the beach   [3] Nicole
[4] The dream of the rug   [5] Catrine's death   [6] Time with Wiana   [7] The attempt at suicide

1954	*1955*	*1956*
29 March 23:30		
10 April 17:00		
22 November 17:00		

1960	*1961*	*1962*
4 January 17:30	12 February 13:00	24 January 15:30
5 January 20:00	19 July 11:00 (2)	4 May 21:00
6 January 9:00	22 July 11:00	13 May 9:00
28 March 18:00	26 July 10:00	18 September 15:00
15 August 12:00 (2)	10 November 20:00	21 September 10:30
1 September 13:00	11 November 14:00	24 September 16:00[2]
	23 November 18:15	4 October 15:00
		5 October 12:00
		17 October (night)
		22 October 7:45
		23 October 12:00 (2)
		24 October 6:00 (2)
		24 October 17:30

1966	*1967*
1 January 2:00	1 January 4:00
2 January 0:30	4 January 19:30[5] (5)
8 January 17:00 (2)	
10 January 15:00	5 January 8:00
1 September 15:00 (2)	5 February 23:00
5 September 16:00	8 February 11:00
(numerous)	4 March 24:00[6] (5)
7 September 16:00	5 March 13:55 (2)
2 September 13:00 (2)	6 March 5:00 (2)
11 October 21:00	1 August (night)
31 December 22:00	3 August (night)
	5 August 5:00[7]
	27 August 12:00
	31 August 12:45
	3 September 16:00

the exigencies of the experiment: the return to the sea, exactly one year earlier.

Monday, 5 September 1966, 4 p.m. Ridder has been snorkling. He is leaving the water. It drips off him. The sound of the drips rises in pitch as their volume decreases. This will become a refrain of the film. The first time he plunges into the past we only see him leaving the water. Then we are, suddenly, back in the 'sphere'. Ridder is there. He disappears. We see him swimming in the water, towards us: a moment earlier than the previous plunge into the past. The sphere again. He appears. He disappears. The beach. Ridder leaving the water (again).

CATRINE: Was it nice?

Ridder swimming towards us again. Ridder walking towards the water.

RIDDER: You coming?
CATRINE: Later!

Ridder leaving the water.

RIDDER: Two sea serpents, several sharks, some giant jellyfish. Apart from that, nothing in particular.

Ridder under water. Swimming towards us. The sound of his measured breathing heavy on the soundtrack. Ridder in the sphere. He appears. He disappears. Ridder leaving the water.

CATRINE: Was it nice?
RIDDER: Very.
CATRINE: Did you see a lot of fish?
RIDDER: Two sea serpents, several sharks, some giant jellyfish. Apart from that, nothing in particular.

The effort to put that small experience together, to make it whole and chronological, weighs on audiences with a unique pressure. Resnais is doing nothing less than asking us to give up preconceptions of causality and the flow of time.

Ridder will return again and again to that precise moment, exactly a year earlier. His movement out of the water, the sound of the water dripping, Catrine's question and his answer will take on the aura of an involuntary ritual: trapped in the eternal moment. I think it's no accident that Ridder catches himself swimming. The return to the sea is a useful metaphor and the act of swimming comes closest to duplicating in everyday life the experience of Ridder's trip. He is close to the state of sensory deprivation in the sphere. He has only his own mind to depend on. That will kill him if neither the machine nor the gun does.

'You coming?' 'Later!' 'Was it nice?' 'Very!' The sphere. The water. His

7–22. Sunday, 5 February 1967, in the Chinese restaurant with his friends Bernard and Marcelle Hannecart (Bernard Fresson, Irène Tunc). In a longer version of this brief scene cut from the final print of the film, Ridder lies to his friends, who don't yet know about Catrine's death, that he has decided to leave her, as they've long suggested. Resnais may have cut it because it adds a little too much to the illusion that Ridder was directly responsible for Catrine's death.

7–23. Monday, 5 September 1964, 1:30 p.m. Ridder waits for a tram in a suburb of Brussels. It is one of the seemingly superfluous moments in his life that has taken on some kind of symbolic meaning.

7-24. Thursday, 23 November 1961, 6:15. Publisher's office. Ridder is correcting proofs by telephone. As an editor, Ridder has spent his professional life pruning, correcting, and rearranging other people's fictions and facts. Now, he has a chance to rearrange his own past.

travelling companion, the mouse beside him in the sphere, appears. Disappears. 'Was it nice?' 'Very! Did you see a lot of fish?' 'Two sea serpents . . .' It's the film editor's nightmare. It's also irresistible: a litany of lives in the living. *Je t'aime, je t'aime* is a highly sensuous film, much denser and richer an experience than a straight narrative could be.

The freedom from time that *Je t'aime, je t'aime* forces upon us not only allows us to savour the shards of Claude Ridder's broken life with special gusto, but also provides a useful irony. In a cerebral way, *Je t'aime* is a very humorous film. Resnais was most disappointed that audiences in general did not catch on to this aspect of the experience. 'It's very ironical', he suggests, ' – with a lot of sadness, that's true – but I would have preferred to hear people laugh more.'[5] There are some magnificent jokes in the film, and the whole tenor manages to attenuate the stark alienation of Ridder's life considerably. Here, for example, is Claude at work in his warehouse, Monday, 22 November, 1954:

RIDDER: Paradis.
EMPLOYE: Bauweleers. Tirlemont.
RIDDER: Ombre.
EMPLOYE: Bauwalincks. Mons.
RIDDER: Paradis.

EMPLOYE: Bauwens, Wolume Saint Pierre.
RIDDER: Galie.
EMPLOYE: Bauwens, Wiels, Malines.
RIDDER: Paradis.
EMPLOYE: Bauweraerts. Bruges.
RIDDER: Lumière.

Joycean poetry out of the strange language of Flemish. The film is studded with puns and wordplay, much of it difficult to translate. Ridder is on the edge. Back in October 1962 in the office one afternoon he muses lugubriously:

It's three o'clock in the afternoon. Still three hours to get by. In three weeks it will still be three o'clock. In a century, too. Time's passing for others, but for me alone, enclosed in this room, it doesn't pass any more. I'm out of the game, out of time. It will always be three o'clock (*He picks up the phone to make a call.*) Hello!. . .Hello! . . . .Is this time? (*The sound of the signal beeps.*) I'm going to tell you that at the third stroke it will be exactly 3 o'clock, no minutes, and no seconds. What? . . .to be sure! sure! Tomorrow, same time, as usual. My regards.

Only Ridder can scold time. Actually, he has missed an hour. For him it is going to be an eternal 4 p.m. Or a beach. Or Catrine. The three coordinates of his trip.

7–25. The final image of the film. The mouse in his plastic hemisphere reaches for the air. As Sternberg describes it in the script: 'She looks in good health, she's enjoyed her trip.' It was very nice.

143

Resnais has moved from a cinematic universe in which form tyrannises characters, through a realistic world in which characters have the power of decisions and indecisions, to a hyperhuman system in which decisions are beside the point. Everything exists. Always.

It is not an easy world to enter with him. But the life that montage can give is singular and profoundly ingratiating. [*Was it nice? Very.*]

8. Projections: The Nonfilms

Like most directors who develop their own projects rather than taking assignments from producers, Alain Resnais has been plagued by a peculiar, yet endemic, occupational hazard: the 'nonfilm'. He has prepared almost twice as many films as have eventually reached the screen during the last twenty years. Some of these projects never got past the discussion stage, but a number of them reached the point of finished scripts. A few, like the adaptation by Frédéric de Towarnicki of the popular serial of the twenties, *Les Aventures d'Harry Dickson*, by Jean Ray, have become legends. In the great majority of cases, the scripts remain unfilmed because Resnais and his collaborators have not been able to convince producers to put up enough money. But financing isn't the only problem; in a few cases Resnais abandoned projects that were well along in development simply because he lost interest, or because he felt that he was not the right man for the job.

This is not an unusual situation in film today. Since few directors are any longer under contract, and since much of the work of production is done by numerous small companies and individuals, a filmmaker finds it more time-consuming to set up each project. Whereas the Hollywood craftsmen of the thirties and forties made as many as three films a year, under contract, and therefore had a chance to experiment and to fail without damaging their reputations, contemporary filmmakers are notoriously only as 'bankable' as their last films. Of course, they also enjoy far more artistic freedom, but very often this liberty expresses itself as freedom not to make films.

Je t'aime, je t'aime was not a great success commercially and partially as a result it was slightly more than six years before Resnais's next film, *Stavisky...*, premiered in May 1974. Received opinion has it that Resnais is a director of what are still known in producing circles as 'art films', yet it wasn't only his marginal commercial appeal that was responsible for the hiatus. Much of the American money that had been flowing into European film production during the middle sixties dried up about the time Resnais was trying to finance

8–1. Resnais has been interested in Harry Dickson, the pulp 'American Sherlock Holmes' since at least the forties. Here, in *Toute la mémoire du monde*, he paid homage to him.

the successor to *Je t'aime*. Even a proven commercial director like Richard Lester (whom Resnais admires) found it impossible to put together a film to direct during this period. For Lester, who had made more than $50 million for United Artists in the mid-sixties with four films, the drought lasted for five years after the disastrous box-office reception of *The Bed-Sitting Room* in 1968. The withdrawal of American capital from European production coupled with the recession of the early Nixon years marked an end to the period of expansion in the sixties which is generally known as the New Wave. Resnais in the seventies is operating in an entirely different context, as we shall see.

Of course, he did not know at the time that it would be five years before he got behind a camera again. In retrospect he looks on the period 1969–73 as one of the busiest in his career, ironically. 'The funny thing was that I was so afraid that taking a vacation would jeopardize a project that I did not take any for four years. I have the feeling that I have worked more than ever during those four years!'[1] Partly with an eye on the increasingly necessary American market, and partly just because he enjoyed it, much of this period was spent in New York. He enjoyed the city, spending a year there in 1970 and 1971, and the experience partially made up for the inactivity. 'It's more fun to wait for money in New York than Paris,' Resnais puts it.

Although one never thinks of film directors as being penurious, Resnais has always lived frugally, and the greatest problem during this period was simply finding money to live on. 'I was very worried, because it's impossible to survive just asking friends to lend you money. It's very depressing.' He wasn't especially worried about the fact of not financing the projects he developed during this period because they were all very expensive. 'If I could have found a script that could have been made for less than half a million dollars,' he concludes, 'and nobody cared to produce it, then I would have felt that there was a curse.'

As we've already noted, the pattern of nonfilms was long established with Resnais. There were a number of false starts on features in the fifties before

8–2. Resnais made a number of trips to London, beginning in 1948, during which he shot still studies for a future film about Harry Dickson. This one dates from a period during which the film appeared possible. These studies, together with most of the photographs in this chapter, come from a book Resnais published in 1974 with a long introduction by Jorge Semprun. The title of this collection of remarkable photographs was *Repérages*. The word means locating, marking, logging, or citing, and is also used to refer to the synchronization of sound and image in film. Semprun, in his introduction, suggests the pun with 'reparer' is significant. To some extent these images from lost films are 'reparages'.

Hiroshima mon amour. During the sixties, in addition to the legendary Harry Dickson project, there were attempts at a film based on *La Permission*, a novel by Daniel Anselme, and an original script, *A Suivre à n'en plus finir*, by Anne-Marie de Villaine before Resnais turned to *Marienbad.* As he has often said, 'one doesn't make the films one wants to make, one only makes those one is allowed to make'.

There is no greater proof of the truth of this observation than the history of Resnais's nearly forty year quest for the mysterious Harry Dickson.* He had run across issues of the serialized adventures of 'le Sherlock Holmes américain' (as Dickson was advertised) in Vannes in the early thirties. He was fascinated by the complexity of the character, who combined elements of the supremely logical Holmes stories (although American, Dickson lived a few doors away from Holmes on Baker Street) with supernatural fantasy milieus of the sort Resnais had become acquainted with from Breton folklore.

Over the years, he gradually built up a complete collection of the 178 episodes of the adventures of the mysterious pulp hero. At first, there was no thought of a film version of the Dickson saga. Resnais visited London for the first time in 1949 and immediately searched out and photographed the quickly disappearing sites of his hero's exploits. Three years later, the plan for a film first took shape. There was one seemingly insurmountable problem, however. The author of the Dickson series had never been identified, and now, the Belgian publisher had disappeared. Finally, after many false leads, a second-hand bookseller informed Resnais that the anonymous author was one Jean-Raymond de Kremer, who wrote in Flemish as John Flanders, and in French as Jean Ray. A retired sailor, he lived in Ghent. Resnais finally met him in 1959.

The history of the Dickson saga was even more intriguing. The Belgian publisher had originally hired Kremer/Ray around 1930 to do some translations of a complete set of detective stories he had just bought from a German publisher. Very quickly, Kremer became disenchanted with the insipid plots he had to put into French and worked out an agreement with the publisher that would allow him to rewrite the stories completely (but still anonymously). The only caveat was that the Belgian publisher couldn't afford new covers, and so Kremer/Ray's new stories had, in some way, to relate to them.

The result was, then: a series of pulp adventures, part translated, mainly invented, first written in German, then French, by a writer at home in both Flemish and French, about an American hero who lived in England, and set in a confused timeless era which was part 1930s, part 1890, part 1905, and part 1914.

By 1960, Resnais had a completed script of 'Les Aventures d'Harry

* Well-documented by Francis Lacassin in the Autumn 1973 issue of *Sight and Sound*.

Dickson', but it would have run four hours, and in addition, it was proving impossible to find an actor who could properly play the role who was also acceptable to potential producers. Between 1960 and 1967 (when, after every film, Resnais was announcing that his next project would be 'Harry Dickson') the script was shortened three times. By the end of 1967, Resnais had got it down to a manageable two hours but – Francis Lacassin reports – wasn't happy with the results. 'A series of fascinating fragments, but only fragments, and I couldn't find an ending,' Resnais said. During the past ten years, Jean Ray's fantasies have been republished to some acclaim, but the film Resnais has had in mind for more than 25 years remains a wish.

Resnais's first project in New York during the late sixties was an ambitious 'essay' on the Marquis de Sade in collaboration with editor and translator Richard Seaver. He spent a year on it in 1969–70, and got to the point where he had a commitment from Dirk Bogarde to play the Marquis and a finished and revised script: 'Délivrez-nous du bien', but the project couldn't be sold. He moved on to a totally contrasting idea for a film to be written by Stan Lee, the originator of Marvel comics. This took another year, with only slightly better results. 'The Monster Maker' was sold to Martin Ransohoff's Filmways company. But there it died on the shelf.

This was followed by an idea for a documentary on the life of H. P. Lovecraft, the fantasy writer of the twenties and thirties. William Friedkin and Warner Brothers *seemed* to be the backers, but after all, nothing happened, and William Friedkin had to begin shooting *The Exorcist'*. At about the same time, Resnais explored the possibility of doing a film of Penelope Mortimer's novel *The Home* with equal results. But let Mortimer describe their collaboration:

I first met Resnais in June 1972, when he and his wife had been living for a year in New York. He gave me the impression then of a lean man, impeccably dressed in cashmere and (I think) denim. He looked hungry. All visiting Europeans in New York, in my experience, look hungry. They probably are. I was supposed to write a screenplay from one of my novels, which he was supposed to direct. The suppositions were, of course, part of the mythology of the movie business. We frequently sat on couches, drinking coffee and listening to the co-producers arguing about the casting of unwritten parts. Occasionally we would meet in the garden of the Museum of Modern Art and very quietly, almost conspiratorially, discuss the characters for whom the parts had yet to be written. The film, I need hardly add, never got made. It turned out there wasn't enough money to buy a typewriter ribbon, let alone employ Elizabeth Taylor: at the mention of whose name Resnais would somehow manage to look even hungrier, almost wraithlike, as though he were attempting to become invisible.[2]

As Resnais put it, more succinctly, 'the producer gave – how you call a cheque when it bounce? – a "bad cheque".' That was *The Home*.

8–3. Resnais in New York. [Photo by Olivier Rebbot, Gamma Agency]

By this time Resnais had given up on New York and had returned to Paris. Jorge Semprun first mentioned the idea for *Stavisky...* to Resnais in 1972. But even though it was relatively easy this time to raise the money, on the strength of Jean-Paul Belmondo's name, it still took Semprun more than a year to complete the script. It's good to remind oneself once in a while, how very long it takes to make a film. A 10-week shooting schedule is only the tip of the iceberg.

While he was working with Semprun on *Stavisky...* and later during the period of preparation for *Providence* (which was an unusually quick project for Resnais), two more potential films began to gestate. As I write, there is no way of knowing whether or not they will be stillborn or eventually reach the screen. One of these was a longtime dream of Resnais's, a film part documentary and part fiction on Henri Laborit's theories of the biochemical processes of the brain – a kind of gloss on the machine of *Je t'aime* if you will. At various times, Jorge Semprun and Jean Gruault worked on the script, whose working titles have included, 'Ile' and 'Mon Oncle d'Amérique'.

The other recent project has been a second film with Stan Lee, 'The Inmates', which is equally apocalyptic in an entirely different way. Lee describes it as

8–4, 5. Repérages in New York for 'The Inmates'. Semprun, in his introduction to the collection of Resnais's photos suggests that all the images, usually empty of people, or glimpsing a solitary figure lost in the landscape, whether shot in London, Paris, Hiroshima, or New York, be considered as studies of an imaginary cinematic city. He names that city 'Arkham', in homage to H. P. Lovecraft.

a science fiction qua love story based on the concept that the human race has, in fact, been quarantined on earth and other beings are therefore not allowed to contact us. A crisis develops; for various reasons the powers that be may have to destroy us. The form, however, is personal rather than cosmic: a love story between two people, a woman extraterrestrial and a man who is native to earth. By mid-1977, Lee had completed a detailed treatment for the film.

As it happens, one gets a much better sense of Alain Resnais's developing interests during the last ten years from an examination of these nonfilms than from an analysis of the two films he did complete. Those were the films he was 'allowed' to make, and only tangentially related to the films he 'wanted' to make. If we survey the projects as well as the completed films, for example, one of Resnais's main interests is obviously the literature of popular culture. He grew up, of course, with an avid interest in comic books and pulp serials and the long unrealized project of 'Harry Dickson' and the two collaborations with Stan Lee attest to a still abiding fascination with those forms, as does the idea for the film on H. P. Lovecraft.

Yet of the films actually made, only *Je t'aime, je t'aime* and *Stavisky...* reveal any evidence of these influences – and they do so tangentially. The science fiction framework of *Je t'aime* may seem peripheral, but Resnais explains, perhaps a bit too self-effacingly, 'I like pulp literature, and so I thought it was fun to have the film beginning as a B movie – or a Z movie – like a kind of bad serial, but maybe that was a little too perverted.'[3] Likewise, *Stavisky...* is thoroughly grounded in Resnais's knowledge of the way the popular press treated the legend of the man in the thirties. Precisely, *Stavisky...* is not about the historical character, Resnais warns, but about the way in which that character was seen through the colour supplements.

Yet most audiences can easily ignore this pop culture aspect of both *Je t'aime* and *Stavisky...*, while in the unrealized projects that theme is unavoidable.

At the other extreme is the narrative abstraction so important to the conception of *Je t'aime*, which seems to have alienated quite a large part of Resnais's audience. Some of this is apparent in *Providence*, but as we shall see, once again audiences can overlook this with impunity. The scripts for 'Délivrez-nous du bien' and, one imagines from Resnais's description, for the project on Henri Laborit explore new ways of storytelling in such a way that audiences would have been (will be) forced to consider them. If Resnais had access to unlimited production funds with no strings attached, our image of his world would be markedly different.

Richard Seaver, a well-known editor and translator of most of the Marquis de Sade's works into English, spent much of the fifties in Paris running a small

8–6. Richard Seaver

literary magazine called *Merlin* and a publishing enterprise that released such books as Beckett's *Watt* and Genet's *Our Lady of the Flowers*, in addition to de Sade. As a sideline, he also acted as advance scout for American film importers. Ironically, however, he did not meet Resnais until he moved back to New York in the late fifties. A mutual friend, Delphine Seyrig, introduced them during Resnais's first trip to the U.S. in 1960. Resnais and Seaver eventually became close friends.

They discovered that they shared a fascination for de Sade and, on one of the Seavers' trips to Paris in 1967 or 1968, Resnais suggested 'why don't we do a film on de Sade?' Seaver had never thought of himself as a screen-writer, but the possibilities interested him. Resnais, he says, told him he would call him in a month to find out how the treatment was going. 'On the thirty-first day after I left Paris,' Seaver continues, 'the phone rang and it was Alain and he said "your month is up".'[4] Seaver hadn't accomplished much in the allotted time. 'The problem was the vastness of the project.' But eventually, after Resnais had moved to New York in 1969, they were able to work out the ground rules. During one weekend that summer, according to Seaver, 'we got the whole structure of the film'. With a better conception of what the film might look like, Resnais returned to France and spent at least a month scouting locations and photographing them in detail; a process, Seaver says, he follows with most of his films.

Meanwhile, Seaver set to work collecting and creating the dialogue to fill the structure they had conceived. When Resnais returned, the by now familiar process of consultation began. Having translated most of de Sade, Seaver had excellent recall of various useful passages. The problem was that de Sade had written far too much. As with Sternberg several years earlier, Resnais was confronted with an editing job before the film was shot. The version of the script as it now exists after several revisions still runs two and a half hours, which Seaver thinks is too long.

'Délivrez-nous du bien' is a torrent of words and images that attempts an evocative portrait of an artist – and a man – both Seaver and Resnais were obsessed with. It borrows from *Je t'aime, je t'aime* the basic device of a nonchronological narrative, but because it is about such a towering historical character – and a writer into the bargain – it is a much more powerful and ambitious script. While the basic saga of de Sade is communicated through a violent montage of images taken nonchronologically from the course of his adult life (as in *Je t'aime*), at the same time these images are tensely opposed to de Sade's own voice, incessant on the soundtrack, narrating – pleading, cajoling, explaining, apologizing, ranting, begging, cursing, fantasizing, rationalizing, soothing, dreaming, and calling us to heartfelt revolutionary action.

The effect is extraordinary. It is a condensed summary of de Sade, a writer who suffered from logorrhoea, as well as more colourful afflictions, and who therefore benefits tremendously from this distillation process. When and if the film is made, it will crystallize and codify de Sade's influence for a generation. Resnais and Seaver wisely let de Sade speak for himself. The film is controlled by his point of view and nearly all the narrative (with certain marked exceptions) is taken directly from de Sade's voluminous writings. As Seaver said, the main problem was to boil the script down to manageable proportions. Often, in discussing a scene, they hit upon similar passages which made the point a little more effectively. 'So in an earlier version the scene might be out of *Justine*, while in a later version out of *Letter From the Bastille*.'

The soundtrack narrative, because it is so deeply rooted in de Sade, is unusually powerful in and of itself. The images Resnais and Seaver have sketched out (in considerable detail, compared with most scripts) would work dialectically with de Sade's apologia, sometimes reinforcing his narration, sometimes opposing it.

In addition, Seaver and Resnais (like most of Resnais's collaborators, Seaver finds it difficult to remember who suggested what) have devised several

8–7. Repérage for 'Délivrez-nous du bien'. The ruins of the marquis's chateau at Lacoste. 'On one of the rocks,' Resnais writes, 'you can still see the signature of André Breton, written in red lipstick.'

8–8. Repérage for 'Délivrez-nous du bien'. Vénasque.

8–9. Repérage for 'Delivrez-nous du bien'. Isle-sur-Sorgue. 'De Sade saw it.'

other narrative techniques to help them keep de Sade under nominal control. Much of the film would have been shot on an elaborate set built on wooden underpinnings; Resnais and Seaver intended occasionally to stage scenes or parts of scenes off the realistic sets on these foundations to 'rupture the historical illusion'. The device seems somewhat irrelevant to me, and it is not clear whether or not the final film would have included such shots, but Seaver seems to think that Resnais 'has a constant need to break illusion'.

For the most part, the film is a battle between the voice of de Sade and the images which illustrate or contradict it. As a dialectic between image and sound it rivals Godard's efforts in the same area in the late sixties and early seventies. De Sade's isn't the only voice we hear; scenes are played out on occasion between characters in a realistic mode; but his is the only voice in the film that has the power to control the image. As Seaver puts it in his 'Statement of Intentions' for the film, the other characters 'will have no right to present their side of the story visually. Their only arm of attack (or defence) is verbal. If this seems one-sided, remember that de Sade is one and they are many – a whole society.'

De Sade's adversaries – his wife, his son, his mother-in-law; Laurent, his opposition in the Piques Assembly; Marais, his legal nemesis; Massé, the printer who betrayed him; and numerous others – are allowed to speak their case, but only 'in portrait', as the script puts it. That is, talking while they are on screen, directly to the camera.

Meanwhile de Sade's voice dominates the film to such an extent that it is never really absent. 'Although it will be interrupted on occasion,' Seaver writes,

it will continue speaking at most times even while the others speak, as a whisper or a murmur beneath their words. Even when it is silent beneath others' words, one may well have the impression that it is still going on.[5]

It is incessant, and haunting, and while it is occasionally coordinated with the image of de Sade on the screen, it still dominates that image. The narrator's voice drifts imperceptibly into the character's voice (both de Sade) but the quality is different. It is as if de Sade were speaking with himself – or allowing himself to speak.

This is just the point Seaver and Resnais want to make. For them, the fascination with the character stems from his own remarkable self-analysis. The 'Statement of Intentions' again:

An outsider, a 'loner', de Sade quickly assessed the strictures and hypocrisies of the society into which he was born and decided to have none of it. He also by slow degrees assessed his own psychic make-up, his fears and obsessions, compulsions and anxieties, and from that self-analysis constructed not only a mode of living but a whole philosophical system, a full century before Freud.

In order to emphasize this self-created quality, Seaver and Resnais have developed elaborate and – at least in the script – quite stunning fantasy images to do justice to the egregiousness of de Sade's imagination. In an extension of the technique in *Je t'aime* (which was so muted there as to go almost unnoticed), the images of the film operate on several levels: in the past but also in the present; as objective truth or as distorted truth (that is, as de Sade imagined something happened or as he would have wanted it to happen); or as straight fantasy.

De Sade's fantasies, to say nothing of objectively portrayed episodes from his life, were to have a noticeable shock effect in the late sixties, just at the period when film was being expanded into fields of erotic fantasy and pornographic realism. Seaver and Resnais were very careful to control as far as was possible any prurient interest the film may have had. What was most shocking about it, they thought, was the cool matter-of-factness of its tone. Now they both think the film's potentially erotic material might be dated. That seems to me far from the truth. It might not evoke the kind of outcry now that it would have before *Deep Throat*, *Sweet Movie*, *Salò*, and the genre of not so overtly sexual violence which dominates movie screens in the seventies and comes close to fulfilling de Sade's most outrageous fantasies. But 'Délivrez-nous du bien' would still capture the tenor of the neurotic dreams of the Marquis de Sade, and that would be quite enough to quench any talk of its being dated.

The film begins with de Sade's logical premise, couched in the idiom of Samuel Beckett, a salute to another Seaver hero. De Sade's voice begins in fragments, 'not unlike a distant radio station':

... given I say the non-existence ...
... the figment the figment of our poor lustreless imaginations ...
... the man who wears a blindfold wilfully ...
... to set, I say, to set the record straight, provide evidence, show facts ...
... given the non-existence as uttered forth in the works of d'Holbach, given, I say ...
... the non-existence of a personal god, of any god whatsoever, that which is naught but the figment of our poor lustreless imaginations, the product of fear, it therefore follows as the day the night ...
... that he who continues to believe in the existence of the chimerical creature is like the man who wears a blindfold wilfully, and when the priest says to me, Atheist, you are lost, there is no restoring the blind to the light, I reply that of the two, he who blindfolds himself and he who snatches the blindfold from his eyes, the former must surely see less of the light than the latter.

For priests and the pious erect and multiply, whereas I destroy, I simplify. Priests add error to error, I combat them all. Which one of us then is blind? ...

Seaver has divided the script into four sections, or 'acts'. The first act gives us most of the elements of the history of de Sade. The long years in prison, his attitude towards death, the testy relationships with relatives, the quality of his affairs with women ... the locales, the characters, and the lineaments of his philosophy. It focuses on the connections between de Sade and his wife, and de Sade and his mother-in-law, Madame de Montreuil. Pervading everything is his paranoid yet righteous defence of himself in the face of social hypocrisy.

Act Two elaborates on de Sade's crimes and his fantasies, then settles down to a hypnotic vision of his philosophy:

They have made me dream of crimes so great, so all-encompassing, that the world would tremble to hear them, would blush with shame to learn they had been committed by one of their own species. I dream of a crime whose effect would be perpetual so that there would not be a moment in my life, waking or sleeping, when I was not the cause of some chaos so great that its effects would still be felt long after my death ...

Act Three focuses exclusively on de Sade's period of freedom during the revolution and his consequent attempt at practical politics rather than abstract basic mode of discourse of 'Délivrez-nous du bien' and Resnais must have philosophy. De Sade is tried and dismissed from his post as leader of the Piques Assembly. He has been tried earlier for various crimes. Trials are the basic mode of discourse of 'Délivrez-nous du bien' and Resnais must have found the metaphor to his liking since trials also play central symbolic roles in both *Stavisky...* and *Providence*.

Act Four is built around de Sade's death and the period leading up to it at Charenton. Within this framework, Seaver repeats the themes which had been introduced earlier (especially in the longest section, Act One) and finishes off the mood of the film. It closes with a very long, very slow tracking shot backwards from a closeup of 'de Sade motionless in his chair. He is ancient now, mummylike, such as we glimpsed him once before at the first intrusion into his cell. As the Voice goes on reciting the litany of his arrests we move slowly away . . . .' The effect is stunning. Both Seaver and Resnais were curious as to why such mild-mannered men as themselves found such fascination in the work of the Marquis de Sade. The film goes a long way to explaining the attraction, which concerns not so much the strict psychological aberration which now bears his name, but rather a more purely intellectual power, no less remarkable for being more abstract and less horrendous.

De Sade, in effect, created himself. His literary image of himself supersedes and overwhelms his historical acts. As we know him now, he was a profoundly self-imagined man. The real person, despite his crimes and aberrations, was of little importance, but what de Sade did with that material in his writings is riveting. Seaver has written a script not about characters, events, and conclusions, but about a literary Voice of fearful power. And the unusual confluence of word and image which is outlined in 'Délivrez-nous du bien' manages, I think, to capture the distinct power of the Voice with furious clarity.

Stan Lee's 'The Monster Maker' is as different from 'Délivrez-nous du bien' as it is possible to be. Much less of what would have been the eventual film is evident in the written text. Although it seems more popular in orientation than Seaver's script, it is in a strange way less commercial. With a little bad luck, it could easily have been a disaster for Resnais, for it depends far more heavily on execution, on *mise en scène*, than the de Sade film. Its structure is very simple; it reads like nothing so much as a comic book. Yet Resnais and Lee were planning an effect which is measurably more difficult than complicated narrative structure: this naive, comic-book story was going to be shot with a subtle tone of cinematic irony to be a commentary on the style as well as an example of it. We've already noted that it was this line of development Resnais was to follow in the film that did get made, *Stavisky...* . But in *Stavisky...* the experiment is a safe one, since audiences can easily overlook that ironic, self-referential tone. Not so with 'The Monster Maker'.

Stan Lee is best known as the creator of the Marvel Comics group. The

8–10. Stan Lee

Marvel heroes – among them Spider-Man, The Hulk, Thor, The Silver Surfer – have supernatural powers on the model of the classic Superman and Captain Marvel (no relation), but they exercise them in the context of everyday reality. Ordinary people in Marvel comics laugh at these gifted grotesques, and they suffer neurotically for it. The Fantastic Four, the original Marvel heroes, for example, can get evicted for not paying their rent. Or the leader of the group can invest their reward money in bad stocks and lose it all. There's an insouciance and realism to the Marvel style Lee created that verges on satire and has attracted a generation of children who continue reading the books into adulthood.

Resnais first met Lee through his interest in comics. Lee has told the story many times, polishing it in the process:

What happened was, Fellini came up to see me. I thought it was a joke. The girl said, 'Stan, somebody named Fellini here to see ya.' I said, 'What's his first name?' 'Just a minute.' She came back a minute later: 'Federico.' I said, 'Aw, come on!' Anyway, I wanted to see what the gag was so I said show him in. And sure enough in comes Fellini with an entourage of about five other people and they walk in in descending order of height. It was very funny. And he's wearing a black coat over his shoulders, his arms not through the sleeves. (I don't think an Italian director would be caught dead with his arms in the sleeves of his coat.) As I remember, the other five guys were also wearing black coats. Anyhow, we talked for a couple of hours and he said he had been a big fan of Marvel Comics and of mine and I was very impressed with myself. I was flattered and surprised.

About a year or two later, the girl says, 'Stan, there's a mister Resnais to see you.' Well after Fellini, I figured, it's possible, so I wasn't even surprised. He came in, and he said he would like to take some photos, and he interviewed me. Once again, I was so indescribably flattered. I mean, here's a world-famous director, and he wants to interview me! It was a kick.[6]

Lee and Resnais apparently saw quite a bit of each other while Resnais was in New York. Resnais, according to Lee, was particularly fond of a nondescript coffee shop on Third Avenue for lunch. He also ate often in Chinatown. Stan learned to use chopsticks.

At one point – and this is the way Lee tells it, you will notice a certain discrepancy – Resnais told him: 'I want my first movie in English to be written by you. I have dreamed that when I finally do a movie in English that you will write my first one.' As ever, it took many conversations to evolve the basic structure of what was to become 'The Monster Maker'. Lee had moonlighted from Marvel writing a number of television and radio soap operas and had been classified as a playwright in the army during World War II, but he found it extremely difficult to work with Resnais. The director never made specific decisions about the script in progress, but through the course of endless discussions his wishes would become irresistible. 'I'm a very fast writer,' Lee claims. 'Working with Alain, I had to go against the grain. All my life I had written just for myself. Now I was trying to please somebody else, as well.'

A seemingly straightforward and simple tale, 'The Monster Maker' involves a producer of grade C horror films, Larry Morgan, with a studio in the Bronx, and his regular crew: Patricia Hill, writer; Stephen Cavanaugh, star; and Nick Romita, director. Having crossed paths with a hot young British film director, Peter Hastings, who has a reputation as an 'artist' and receives adoring tributes at cocktail parties in his honour, Larry is all the more aware of his essential dissatisfaction with himself and his job. He makes good 'C' movies, such as they are, but only children admire his work and look up to him. He has come to a time in his life when he wants more recognition. He also wants to win back his beautiful ex-wife, Catherine Reynolds, who seems to have a crush on Hastings.

At the same time, the actor Cavanaugh's wife has just died. He thinks air pollution was the cause. He goes a little crazy and blackmails Morgan into promising to do a film which will expose the evils of pollution once for all time. Morgan humours him by agreeing.

Having done so with no intention of making the film, Morgan eventually realizes that this 'serious' project might be just the trick he needs to get his

8–11. Repérage for 'The Monster Maker'. Garbage fire near apartment complex in New York.

8–12. Repérage for 'The Monster Maker'. Dead autos looking out to sea.

ex-wife back and gain the world's acclaim. He becomes deeply involved in research, hoping Catherine will write the script. But as Larry becomes more interested in the subject (opportunities here for documentary footage), Catherine loses interest. Eventually it becomes clear the film will not be made.

Stephen Cavanaugh in his sane madness, invokes the wrath of God on Morgan for breaking his promise, and burns down the studio. Larry and Pat catch him at the deed, and after he faints, drive him out to his house in Broad Channel, Queens, a section of New York City which desolately overlooks the great Jamaica Bay swamp. In that lugubrious setting, Pat and Larry find true love:

PAT: I told you that everyone lives with his own private frustration. Well, I'm no exception. The man I really care for doesn't know I'm alive. (*pause*) But, I'm still luckier than most.
LARRY: How?
PAT: At least, I have a chance to be near him – every so often.
LARRY (*puzzled*): Well, then, who – ?
Suddenly he stops, looking at her anew, as comprehension slowly starts to dawn in his eyes. He reaches out, grasping her shoulders, and turns her towards him. Her eyes are tender, soft, slowly growing moist and tearful.
LARRY: Pat. Pat. I never thought, I never even guessed.
He takes her in his arms. She seems to melt, insinuating herself against him. He gently takes her face and cups it in his hands, looking at her slowly, tenderly, as though really seeing her for the very first time.
LARRY: All those months, those years – the time we wasted, because I was too blind.
PAT: (sighing): Larry ...
He bends down to kiss her, the way one would kiss a fragile child.
LARRY: Darling. Darling. We'll never be lonely again.[7]

This, six years before *Mary Hartman, Mary Hartman* showed that parody of the reigning soap opera style could be profitable as well as artistically successful. The model for 'The Monster Maker' is Roy Lichtenstein's pop art parodic style. The film would have been, if all went right, Resnais's great comic success.

But the film does not end on this note of eternal and timeless true love conquering all, *Modern Romance* style. The Monster has yet to be heard from! The next morning, Larry's car won't start. Garbage blocks the wheels. And Stephen is missing. They trace him to a deserted island in the bay. Stephen's reign of terror has begun. The sky darkens with smoke. The bay overflows with pustulous flotsam and jetsam – and worse – dreck. Garbage runs rampant in the streets. In a montage of 25 extraordinary scenes, pollution triumphs in the city as crowds run screaming in terror from the stench, the smoke, the horror of it all.

8–13. Repérage for 'The Monster Maker'. An automobile graveyard near a middle-class neighbourhood in New York. The smog hangs in a thin line just above the scene.

8–14. Repérage for 'The Monster Maker'. Airport, 1970.

8–15. Repérage for 'The Monster Maker'. Landfill project with figures in the landscape. In 1985. New York runs out of available landfill sites.

Just at the last moment, before it is all too late, Stephen walks into the water, to his death. And the terror subsides. The garbage grudgingly recedes, and the air clears. Larry and his beloved Pat breath a collective sigh of relief and walk to their car to ride off into the sentimental future that is their due.

PAT: How, Larry? How? You must tell me. I have to know. How?
LARRY: Don't think about it, darling. It's over. That's all we have to know. Whatever it was – whatever really happened – it's ended. That's all we have to know. It's over, at last.

But, wait! In the last shot of the film 'We see rear wheels of Larry's car as he starts to drive away. A large amount of garbage and litter is starting to accumulate around the wheels and the car's undercarriage. . . .'

'The Monster Maker' is a grand and exuberant compendium of all the clichés of the B movie which have thrilled and enthralled audiences for fifty years: science fiction, sentimental romance, horror, revenge, and cataclysm – it's all there. But more important perhaps, 'The Monster Maker' takes these conventions seriously at the same time as it parodies them. This is not camp, but something more ambitious. Those conventions continue to exist because

8–16. Repérage for 'The Monster Maker'

they serve a need in their audiences, and Resnais and Lee are out to experiment with them to find out why.

The central character, the soulfully self-pitying movie producer Larry Morgan, seems to have been the conception of Stan Lee alone. Resnais was chary, Lee says, of making a film about a filmmaker. Lee admits to similar feelings himself in the period immediately preceding the writing of the script.

The pollution business, which provides such a startling conclusion to the film, on the other hand, was Resnais's idea. Lee never had much interest in the subject. Resnais spent weeks, just as he had with the de Sade film, searching out unusual locations in New York City and photographing them. The montage of scenes of apocalyptic destruction was the result. Both Resnais and Lee were eminently equipped for the job of satirizing popular genres, Lee through practical experience, Resnais through a lifetime of study.

Even Lee wonders whether they could have brought the film off. 'I don't know how that dialogue would have sounded,' he muses. It's an understatement. But whether or not 'The Monster Maker' ever gets made it still serves with 'Délivrez-nous du bien' as striking evidence of the range of Resnais's interests. The films that he has been allowed to make in the present economic system of cinema occupy only small areas on the much broader map of the films that might have been, the nonfilms.

9. The Pyramid

One evening in 1972, Resnais and Jorge Semprun were having dinner together, bringing each other up to date. Since their collaboration seven years earlier on *La Guerre est finie*, Resnais had completed only one film. Most of what he had to tell Semprun, no doubt, had to do with the ironies of the film industry. For Semprun, on the other hand, the last seven years had been quite productive. He had published his second and third novels (*Les Evanouissements* and *La Deuxième Mort de Ramon Mercader*, which won the Prix Femina in 1969) and established a film reputation for himself as one of the leading screenwriters of the day, a reputation which was owed in no small part to *La Guerre est finie*, which had been his first film, but which had been assured, however, by his association with Costa-Gavras. Their *Z* (1969) had become one of the most influential films of the sixties. The second part of the trilogy, *L'Aveu* (*The Confession*, 1970), had not been so popular but was an important statement, nevertheless. *Section Spéciale*, which Costa-Gavras was to film several years later, may have already been in the planning stages. In addition, Semprun had just finished Yves Boisset's *L'Attentat* (1973), a film about the Ben Barka affair, and was already at work on *Les Deux Mémoires*, the first film he would direct himself, a year later. Semprun's luck during the last seven years had been as good as Resnais's had been bad.

At one point, according to Resnais, Jorge turned to him abruptly and said, 'You have never made a second film with the same screenwriter and I want to make a second film with you, just for fun. Is it alright with you?'[1] One can imagine Resnais's emotions. Semprun, whom he had introduced to the film industry, was producing scripts at the rate of one a year. They were getting made. And for the most part they were commercial as well as artistic successes. At this juncture in his life, Resnais may very well have been thinking that he had been too discriminating. Stan Lee tells stories about Resnais and producers that may be apocryphal, yet *se non è vero, è ben trovato*.

'I remember one time,' Lee told me, 'Alain was offered a picture with Ali McGraw and turned it down.' 'No, [Lee affectionately mimics Resnais's French accent] I do not theenk she will be right for eet,' he said. Another time he wanted Laurence Olivier for something and was offered Cary Grant, and turned him down. 'I realized I was dealing with a purist,' Lee concluded. 'He was not gonna sell himself for money!'[2]

But maybe the time had come to make a truce with the Ali McGraws of the world of film.*

Resnais told Semprun: 'Of course it's all right. When do we begin?' But Semprun was busy. 'Maybe in two months,' he replied, 'I have a little thing to write. It will be very easy and we can meet after that.' Resnais became discouraged. He knew that 'in the movie business somebody who thinks that he can write a screenplay in two months is totally mad!' Yet, all was not lost. 'What is the thing you are going to work on?' 'Oh, it's just a thing on Stavisky.' Resnais came back: 'Maybe it's not necessary to wait two months because I am sure that I am quite competent to deal with Stavisky. When I was a kid, 12 years old, I went to the wax museum in Paris and looked at Stavisky in wax.'

At the time, Resnais told himself it was a joke. But his agent called the next day, and said, 'Jorge Semprun told me a strange story that you *could* be interested in this Stavisky picture, is that serious?' Resnais replied, 'Let's try.'

The basic ideas for Resnais's films did not always originate with him, but this was the first time he had come into someone else's project so late. There is other evidence that *Stavisky...* was at least partially a commercial compromise with the exigencies of the film industry of the 1970s. For the first time, for instance, Resnais made use of well-known movie stars and a popular composer to write the music. Semprun was later to joke, 'All Resnais wants to do is make a film starring Belmondo and Boyer, with music by Stephen Sondheim.'[3] Moreover, as an historical film set in the thirties, *Stavisky...* was perfectly set up to take advantage of the art-deco nostalgia which was cresting at just that time, especially since it starred Belmondo, who had foreshadowed the fad for thirties clothes and lifestyles with *Borsalino* (1970), a film named after a hat! Belmondo's presence also made it quite easy to raise the money for the film. In fact, it took only five days to put together financing of $1.5 million (plus Belmondo's salary, a percentage) – not much less than Resnais's 'expensive' American projects would have cost.

Stavisky... certainly succeeded as a commercial commodity. It has been

---

* Ali McGraw was a hot star during the early seventies, mainly because of her role in *Love Story* and her short marriage to Robert Evans of Paramount who prepared *The Great Gatsby* for her, then took the role away from her when the affair broke up.

Resnais's most successful film to date at the box office. It's entertaining, colourful, nostalgic, romantically evocative, and witty and drole. It even has a successful soundtrack album, certainly a first for Resnais. Yet, surprisingly, despite all these obvious commercial elements, it is still quite clearly a film by Alain Resnais, the director of *Marienbad, Muriel, Je t'aime*, and all those cerebral 'art' films of the sixties. It is specious to think that a film can't be intellectually complex just because it is popular. In this respect, *Stavisky...* is Resnais's greatest artistic success, since it reaches out towards mass audiences.

Critically, the film was very well-received in the U.S. and Britain, but, despite its box office success in France (or maybe because of it), *Stavisky...* received a decidedly mixed reception on its home ground. Resnais was charged with 'at the same time saying too much and too little' about his subject, for ignoring the social and political complications that surrounded the Stavisky affair, for lacking conviction, for being too academic, and for paying 'too little attention to historical fact'.

The vituperous nature of these censures surprised both Resnais and Semprun, but the criticisms of the film go straight to its heart. Despite its having occurred forty years ago, the Stavisky affair still excites passions in France and Resnais and Semprun had made their own version of the story, not their critics' version. For most French people, a discussion of Stavisky is unthinkable without detailed attention to the historical events which take place after the period the film covers, after Serge Stavisky's death: The resignation in late January of 1934 of the entire moderate leftist Chautemps cabinet, the fascist riots of 6 February 1934, and the ensuing downfall of the Daladier government together with the emergence of the right-wing National Union cabinet of Gaston Doumergue.

All of this provides necessary background to the film, but Resnais and Semprun don't cover it visually. Part of the reason is that it would have been too expensive to stage the riots. More important, however, at least from the authors' point of view is that Stavisky alive was more interesting to them than Stavisky dead. Since English and American critics had little interest indeed in the political complexities of the Stavisky affair, they took the film on its own terms instead of judging it against their own version of history.

It was imperative for Resnais that the film deal not with the history of Stavisky, which is more muddled than most such stories, but with the legend. The legend was the only thing he knew. Serge Stavisky was for him a product not only of the wax museum (the shooting script for the film includes a scene there near the end which was never shot) but also of the scandal sheets, bicolour weeklies, and gossip columns of the time. They punctuate the film regularly, and the ellipsis of the title indicates the tentativeness of Resnais's and Semprun's portrait. *Stavisky...* is a film about celebrity.

9–1. Resnais, to the left, judiciously observing the image of Stavisky Belmondo is about to project

As in earlier projects, the concept of the film grew and changed as Semprun and Resnais worked on the script. Originally, they had both been intrigued by what Resnais calls 'the mechanism of fraud', how it worked, and how it pervaded society, reaching into the most distant corners of French business and government life. Serge Stavisky depended for his success on the theory of the pyramid, or Ponzi scheme: if 10,000 in fraudulent funds had to be covered, borrow 100,000; if 100,000 had to be supported, raise 1 million; and if that million is lost, steal 10 million to replace it. The pyramid became the metaphorical emblem of the film for Semprun and Resnais: Stavisky was the peak of a structure of fraud that reached deep into the bowels of French society.*

As work on the screenplay progressed, however, Resnais and Semprun discovered that 'little by little, the character was "invading" the picture: and that he was not an ordinary crook, and that his mad love for his wife and his anxiety about old age were after all maybe more interesting than his swindles. The character took over. But it was not at all on purpose. It was a kind of

* A mysterious small stone pyramid appears several times in the film. 'It's one of those irrational but not meaningless elements,' Resnais explains. 'The pyramid is located in the Parc Monceau ... and Stavisky lived near the Parc Monceau.... So one can dream of the young Sacha walking in the park, passing that mysterious pyramid....'⁴

9–2, 3. Precisely, this is a film not about 'Stavisky' but about his creation, Serge Alexandre. (The working title was 'L'Empire d'Alexandre.') Here, in 2, 'Stavisky's' one big scene, Dr. Mézy recounts the story of his arrest 26 July 1926 at Marly-le-roi during an elaborate dinner party. In 3, the new Serge Alexandre speaks to his board of directors.

9–4, 5A. The print media, which were so important in building the legend of Serge Alexandre (and Stavisky) make their appearance early in the film and reappear regularly. In 4, *La Guerre* headlines 'The Gangster Stavisky alias Serge Alexandre and his famous band.' Above the headline, boxed, is a front-page declaration that the paper 'strongly supports the RIGHTS OF JEWS TO LIFE.... But we can't ... defend big jews who, like big catholics or big protestants, EXPLOIT THE LIVES OF OTHERS.' In 5, Baron Raoul reads from *Le Matin* the story of Lord Melchett's conversion to Judaism in protest. Meanwhile, the centre headline focuses attention on Trotsky.

9-6. A mock-up of *Le Petit Journal*, 4 January 1934, prepared especially for the film with Belmondo's and Anny Duperey's portraits. [Courtesy l'Avant-Scène]

9–7. An actual issue of *Le Petit Journal*, with their 'artist's conception' of Stavisky's arrest in 1926. Compare 9–2. [Courtesy l'Avant-Scène]

biological process.'[5] The pyramid then took on value as the metaphor for death and love which is the fabric the film weaves. Freud superseded fraud.

Historically, Serge Stavisky was a brash but erratic conman who moved from skirmishes of a remarkably petty nature in the teens and twenties (stealing theatre tickets, or the gold his dentist father kept for fillings) through ever more elaborate schemes until he re-emerged as 'Serge Alexandre' in the thirties, a theatrical producer, businessman, and financier of such proportions that the shape of his swindles merges, inevitably and imperceptibly with 'respectable' international monetary and political structures. His last scheme posited nothing less then the salvation of Europe from the scourge of the Depression. It was only half a confidence trick.

It's essential to realize the political dimensions of this story. Stavisky, when he fell, brought down with him the French government. As Resnais and Semprun see him he is a model of capitalist man. He may not play the game according to the rules, but the rules are notoriously loose and always changing anyway. For Semprun, Serge Stavisky is the necessary pair to Diego Mora: one an adventurer, the other a militant. He found a text from Sartre which developed the parallel between these two types. It came from the same piece from which was taken the epigraph for *La Guerre est finie*, Sartre's preface to Roger Stéphane's *Portrait de l'aventurier*:

That enormous warehouse filled with merchandise known as bourgeois society will be set ablaze by adventurers, who will, as an ultimate act, throw themselves into the flames. Potlatch, celebration, largesse: these are what will mark their end.[6]

What better précis of the Stavisky story Semprun and Resnais have told? It even makes clear how the character's obsession with his own age and impending death fit into the political structure.

We now have a list of Staviskys of considerable length. Serge Stavisky, the petty confidence trickster who seduces a woman to steal her jewels. Serge Alexandre, the suave image of the scandal newspapers and colour magazines, and an international financier whose network of professional friends and lackeys extends throughout the fabric of French society in the thirties. Sacha, for whom living well is the best revenge. Stavisky the Russian Jew who persists perversely in calling attention to himself in xenophobic, antisemitic France in the early thirties. Alexandre the theoretician of advanced decadent capitalism who explains that 'the only way to attract money is to show it' and who understands probably better than most less successful businessmen of the time that style and image are at least as valuable as cold, hard cash and that cash itself is fictional in nature: credit is all.

We also have Serge the romantic hero whose mad love for his wife Arlette colours everything he does. Alexandre the theatrical producer manqué. Sacha the pre-eminent model of elegance, extravagance, and noble repose who had no trouble disposing of 22 million francs in two years. Then we have the Serge Dr. Mézy describes as schizophrenic and finally the legend Stavisky Resnais and Semprun remember from the media. No wonder the character invaded the story. He was legion.

When the film was released in the U.S., it was often compared (most favourably) with Jack Clayton's and Francis Coppola's *The Great Gatsby.* Most of these comparisons were on the superficial level of style. *Stavisky...* , it was said, succeeded where *Gatsby* had failed in capturing the mood of the era *entre deux guerres.* It does that, of course, but the similarities are deeper. Like Fitzgerald's great American novel (if not the film that was made from it), Resnais's *Stavisky...* gives us one of the last tycoons, the very model of the great self-made capitalist princes of the early years of this century, but seen clearly as a crook. Alexandre, however, is far more intelligent than Fitzgerald's Jay Gatsby. Like Dick Diver, the hero of a later Fitzgerald novel, *Tender is the Night,* Serge knows the value of 'repose', the image of power, the rare characteristic known in the renaissance as 'sprezzatura'. He imagines his own self, and creates it. His life is a very real and powerful fiction. 'All my

9-8. Potlatch, celebration, largesse. Arlette, as the Baron romantically recounts it, poses with Montalvo's Hispano-Suiza at Biarritz. ('... the hydrangeas were in full bloom, that azure blue you love as much as I do.... The sea, but a stone's throw away, with its emerald waves and white foam mingling with the blue of the flowers....')

9–9,10. Arlette (Anny Duperey) and Montalvo (Roberto Bisacco) first as they appear in the Baron's narration, then without the coloration of Baron Raoul's romanticism

9–11, 12. Style, 'repose', 'sprezzatura'. Serge escorts Artlette in black at night, delivers bushels of white flowers of every description to her in the morning just before she wakes

operations are based on credit,' he tells his lieutenant Borelli at one point. 'And where do you think my credit comes from? From the life I lead, that "squandering" you refer to! If I stopped spending my money in public people would begin to grow distrustful. Alexandre must not be doing very well, they'd start to say, and that would be the end of it.' Image is all.

Like Gatsby, too, Stavisky is identified with his amour fou. Both Daisy and Arlette are living metaphors for the root subject of these mythic and apocalyptic stories: the mad fascination of the heroes with money, and the power and style which come with it. It's a Balzacian equation between sexual desire and cold, hard cash. In *Stavisky*... there is the added factor of the setting in time. In the early thirties, this delirious dream of capitalism had reached its absolute zenith. Stavisky was an emblematic supernova; as his star collapsed, so did the dream. Baron Raoul points this up during his testimony at the end of the film when he informs us that the source of the mystical power Alexandre had held over them was his role as the 'herald of death'. His greatest role, the Baron tells us, was as the Ghost in Giraudoux's *Intermezzo*. He was announcing not only his own death, 'not only those of this past February, but the death of an era, of a whole period of history'. These are the concluding words of the film.

When Semprun published a novelization of his script shortly after the film was released he called it *Le Stavisky d'Alain Resnais* – not out of false modesty, I think, but because he wanted to draw attention to the ineluctable fact that this fabric of many Staviskys was, in the end, imagined. In an important sense, Alain Resnais is a character lurking imperceptibly just on the margins of the film, but strictly controlling it. Not to put too fine a point on it, but the film could be said to be not about Stavisky but about Resnais's memories of him. This extra level of narrative irony was not a factor in any of Resnais's previous films.

In the first place, none of the other films were about historical characters, who *could* be remembered or reinvented. In the second, Resnais has admitted many times that he feels himself incapable of dealing with historical periods realistically. The only way for him to make a film about this real person was to approach him through the still-existent myth. The work he had done on 'Délivrez-nous du bien' must have been helpful in this respect. De Sade, too, was an historical character, one which Resnais and Seaver had approached through their image of him rather than through the historical record. As sharply different as the two scripts are, Stavisky and de Sade nevertheless share certain basic characteristics: both are outsiders, de Sade sexually 'perverted', Stavisky economically so. More important, both create themselves, de Sade through his compulsive writings, Stavisky through obsessive attention to the media image he projects. They aren't dead historical characters for Resnais, they're living contemporary myths.

Resnais knew Stavisky through the stories he had read as a child in the popular yellow press, and the style of those journals controls the imagery of the film. It is the closest Resnais has yet come to dealing with the material and effect of the pulp fiction and comic books which so fascinate him, and which he would have been able to investigate in much more detail had he been able to shoot 'Les Aventures d'Harry Dickson' or 'The Monster Maker'.

This popular mode is extended by a parallel with the movies Resnais knows of the period. His original aim had been to make the film in a bicolour process such as was used in the thirties. He thought of *Stavisky...* as a film in 'red and dark brown'. This proved impossible, but he and Sacha Vierny nevertheless spent a good deal of effort in trying to recapture a sense of the style of early thirties movies. They used only setups and shot angles that were possible in the early thirties. Resnais wanted the film to look archaic. To this end, he showed Vierny *Mystery of the Wax Museum*, Michael Curtiz's 1933 film, which had been made in the early bicolour technicolour process. By using a lot of filters they were able to come close to that style. Resnais was very satisfied with the results, at least in the first print, but warns 'it's very difficult to keep control much past the sixth print'.

Acting style was an important factor, as well. Unknown, or realistic actors in the central roles would have suggested a verisimilitude that would have worked against the aims of the film. A well-known star like Belmondo was essential. 'Since we were dealing with a public figure – Stavisky –', Resnais notes, 'the notion of superimposing another public figure – Belmondo – rather intrigued me.' Once that was settled, it was necessary to 'buttress' Belmondo's presence with other 'name actors'. Nor were they asked to act. 'We didn't for one moment set out to try and make people believe that, since we were using actors, they were anything *but* actors.' Resnais had in the back of his mind the way in which Sacha Guitry had played Louis XIV, XV, and XVI. 'He always made the spectator aware that it was he – Sacha Guitry – playing the king.'[7]

Semprun added a few subtle allusions to specific thirties films – Ernst Lubitsch in particular; Resnais convinced Stephen Sondheim to write his first film score, evocative of the music of the period; and the basic structure of the film was complete.

Just as he felt the film couldn't be made without a star like Belmondo to work against the image of Stavisky people remembered, so Resnais felt it was necessary to have a strong melodic score for the picture. 'To give you an idea how important Sondheim's music was to me,' Resnais told Richard Seaver,

9–13-15. Stavisky's death in the newspapers. For *Le Canard Enchainée* it is clearly a suicide. For *l'Humanité*, the government obviously had him killed. *Le Journal* reports only that he was found at Chamonix with a bullet in his head

9–16. The aesthetic politics of stars. Jean-Paul Belmondo, the image of the sixties, versus Charles Boyer, similarly evocative of the thirties. Belmondo versus Stavisky; Boyer versus Baron Raoul.

9–17. Belmondo in repose.

when writing the shooting script I conceived certain key scenes rhythmically, in terms of his music. And on the first day of shooting I had my tape recorder handy, with key passages of *A Little Night Music* constantly in my ear, to make sure that the rhythm of the scene coincided with Sondheim's music.[8]

Resnais made sure the actors' walk fitted Sondheim rhythms. Baron Raoul's gestures were also fitted to the music, and the entire scene with the white aeroplane outside Biarritz was conceived with music in mind.

Like all soundtrack scores in films of this kind, Sondheim's music reinforces the emotions of scenes, but Resnais had another object in mind as well: the melodies, redolent of the thirties, act to distance the legend of Stavisky. They are used only for Stavisky scenes, never for the Trotsky subplot. To make Sondheim's job easier, Resnais had the film videotaped so that the composer could work with it at home, rather than having to spend expensive hours in an editing room which wouldn't have been very conducive. When Resnais and Sondheim first looked at the film together, the director's careful attention to the structure of the music paid off. They were in complete agreement where the music should begin and end.

Resnais knew Sondheim's stage work well, and was an admirer. He was especially influenced by a scene in *Follies*:

At the end there is a very striking scene. Everyone is singing, dancing, and there is John McMartin in a white tuxedo and top hat and just in the middle, everything breaks down, collapses, and the man does not know what he is singing. It is just like he has been struck by death. It made a very violent effect. And I thought, that after all Stavisky was a little bit like this man.[9]

That scene was one of the main models for the mood of the film.

Like Serge Alexandre's schemes and the metaphor of the film, its structure is pyramidal. It builds from a base of mood and atmosphere (more important to *Stavisky...* than to any previous film by Resnais) to a pointed conclusion about the role of the adventurer, 'throwing himself into the flames. Potlatch, celebration, largesse: these are what will mark their end'. Once again, Resnais indicates precise dates and times. Once again, the narrative is built on a five act framework.

The first act takes place on 24 July 1933 in Cassis, Biarritz, and Paris. This day in the life of Serge Alexandre allows the major themes and characters to be introduced within a tight system which emphasizes that this cinematic universe revolves completely around Stavisky. At this point, Alexandre and Arlette are in separate places. Act II takes Serge, Baron Raoul, and Borelli to Biarritz and reunion with Arlette. The trip is as much an escape from business as a journey towards the woman. The third act covers several days in August 1933 and a few more in November of that year leading up to Act IV

9-18, 19. To begin *Stavisky's* first sequence, Resnais tilts down from the flagpole on the roof of the Claridge, then cuts to another shot tilting down from the roof of the lift as it descends. This is the first introduction of Sondheim's theme, which the image matches closely in rhythm.

which concentrates time once again. The main sequence of the act gives us an autumnal trip to the Barbizon forest; Arlette and Alexandre's last romantic journey. Act V begins at the end of December, 1933, and carries us through to Stavisky's death on 8 January 1934.

Interwoven with the straight narrative of Stavisky's last days are three subplots. The first and most obvious concerns the developing storm of nemesis in the persons of Inspector Bonny and Inspector Gardet. Their narratives are almost entirely distinct from Alexandre's throughout. Separate from Bonny's and Gardet's painstaking efforts to catch Stavisky up are the hearing into his death and the subsequent riots that took place in April 1934. Semprun inserts three quick unidentifiable shots of these hearings into the first act. Gradually, they become more numerous and longer, until they dominate the last sequences of the film. The effect is fatalistic, of course. But it also reinforces the basic concept that it wasn't Stavisky's historical existence that counts but the image one had of him. The work of the hearings is to draw a bead on the character. All they succeed in doing is reiterating the complexity and its attendant air of mystery.

Almost entirely separate from the Stavisky story is the most important of the subplots: the sequences which give us a portrait of Trotsky in exile during the last months of Serge Stavisky's life. The film, in fact, begins not

9–20. Inspector Bonny (Claude Rich).

9–21. Erna Wolfgang (Silvia Badesco)

with Stavisky, but with Trotsky's arrival in France on 24 July 1933. Resnais insisted on a subplot like this to give a more precise idea of the time and place in which Stavisky lived. Maurice Chevalier and Mistinguette were considered, along with others, and rejected. Semprun came up with the idea of Trotsky, according to Resnais. His novel *The Second Death of Ramon Mercader* had dealt with Trotsky in exile. The inclusion of the revolutionary was clinched when, reading the investigative report one day, Semprun discovered that a Chief Inspector Gagneux of the Sureté not only made a major report on one Serge Alexandre but had also been the man assigned to keep a close watch on Trotsky. Gagneux became Gardet.

The other parallels between Stavisky and Trotsky were equally important. Both were Russian Jews in a France that was profoundly xenophobic and antisemitic. Both were, eventually, losers. Stavisky's own downfall led circuitously to Trotsky's expulsion from France due to the furore it aroused on the right. And, most important, Trotsky provided the militant presence to be compared with Alexandre's adventurer. Semprun provides a second connection between the two with the character of Erna Wolfgang, the militant German Jew who auditions for Alexandre early in the film, and later falls

186

in with the young radical and admirer of Trotsky Michel Granville. As Silvia Badesco plays her, Erna is a steel-sharp lynchpin for the film. She has worked with Brecht before leaving Germany (her last role was in *The Measures Taken*) and her theories of theatre – and life – are as different from Alexandre's as it is possible to be. She reminds us of the real world outside the Stavisky legend's romance. With Granville, she gives us a future, as well.

For a film that appears to be so commercially seamless and smooth ('It's a film that I made with complete and total nonchalance,' Resnais told his ardent Boswell, Gaston Bounoure, with tongue in cheek) *Stavisky...* has a remarkably precise, carefully thought-out, and detailed narrative structure. It does not wear its complexity on its sleeve, like earlier Resnais films, but that, I think, is all to the good.

To a number of critics of the film, the Trotsky subplot seemed superfluous. Partly, this is because they were treating the film as a simple commercial enterprise, and such weighty historical figures do not belong in star-vehicle entertainments. Partly, it's a reaction against the break in the strong Stavisky story. Yet Trotsky is essential to *Stavisky...* . The militant and the adventurer must be paired. Moreover, both characters were emblems of their time who understood the force of the image of personality: the imagined self. Both recreated themselves: Stavisky invented Alexandre, while Bronstein invented Trotsky. Ultimately, this is the source of the power of *Stavisky...* .

Did Resnais imagine something like the same Sacha/Serge Stavisky/ Alexandre that Stavisky had imagined for his intimate audiences? Of the ten or a dozen books available on Stavisky, Resnais and Semprun depended most heavily on Joseph Kessel's *Stavisky, l'homme que j'ai connu*, published in 1934. Semprun offers a coup de chapeau to Kessel by having Baron Raoul quote his article 'l'appel du sang' on the conversion of Lord Melchett to Judaism as a protest against racial persecution in Germany. When the film was finished, Resnais showed it to Kessel. His response was: 'That's it, that's the way he was. You've really captured the essence of the man.'[10]

They've captured the essence of the time, as well, and the time is not so far removed from our own. Stavisky was not the last of the great capitalist conmen. He remains an excellent model for adventurers.

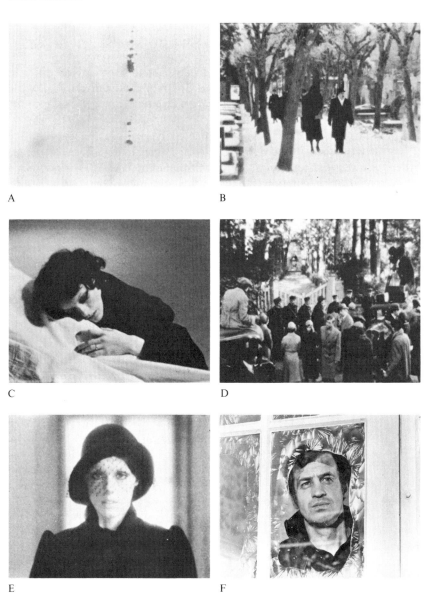

A

B

C

D

E

F

188

G   H

9–22A–H. Shots from the last sequence of *Stavisky...* A. A few drops of bright red blood on white ermine. B. Arlette in black against the white snow of the cemetery. C. Arlette, still in black, against the white shroud. D. The eviction and exile of Trotsky, with the newsreel cameras grinding away. E. Arlette testifying before the committee of investigation. No makeup now, her face sallow and drawn. F. Alexandre framed in the frost of the window of Le Vieux Logis at Chamonix as he sees the gendarmes arriving in force. (Resnais shot at the actual house.) G. Alexandre spends his time in hiding carefully cutting newspaper photographs of Arlette. H. The Baron, in the last image of the film, leaves an extravagant gift of flowers for Arlette at the gate of the prison.

10. The Play of the Drama

'The Scales of Time'

Clive Langham has trouble with his rectum. He is 78, a fairly well-known writer at the end of the line. He spends one nasty night in his Victorian country estate, 'Providence', attempting to deal with his proctological problems, his past, his children, his craft. It is a settling of accounts. Suppositories seem to help him physically; nothing helps psychologically. He is – bluntly – blocked. During the course of the long night, half-asleep, half-drunk, in pain, he spins several dozen scenes using as characters his son Claud, a lawyer; Claud's wife Sonia; and a strange hairy man named Kevin. As Resnais put it, 'He uses his imagination to continue living. If Clive Langham stopped imagining, his body would turn to dust in a few seconds.'[1] Three-quarters of the film *Providence*, written by David Mercer and Resnais's first completed English-language film, is composed of Clive's imaginings, together with his insistent, relentless, testy criticism of them.

The scenes don't work. The backgrounds are imperfectly sketched. The characters are just this side of absurdity. The dialogue is too patly witty for its own good. The story can't be found. There are all sorts of problems. The wrong characters open doors, enter the wrong scenes. They, on occasion, get mixed up in mid scene. Kevin forgets he's Kevin, starts speaking Claud's dialogue. Kevin's younger brother Dave, a football star, has an annoying habit of jogging pointlessly into view just as Clive thinks he might have a lead on a scene. Clive can't make out how to get there or what to do with him. A writer's nightmare. Clive offers excuses to himself and to us:

If one has led a fatuous life, one might as well have fatuous nightmares.[2]

The settings are ludicrous. Claud and Sonia live in a mauve and taupe mausoleum which is breathtakingly effete. Clive can't even keep the details straight. The rooms keep changing from scene to scene. Halfway through the

10-1. John Gielgud as Clive Langham, ever-present bottle of Chablis in hand, photo of Molly on the bedside table.

nightmare (the story, and the film) Clive decides to pair Claud up with a mistress. In his mind's eye, he goes searching for her down an aeroplane aisle. He rejects the first possibility, 'a very attractive girl in jeans and half-unbuttoned shirt':

> Damned if I'm giving you to the dreaded Claud. Could do with you myself. If I could just get off this bed. Out of this coffin of a room.

He settles for an older woman, still attractive. But the imagination is weak. The mistress Helen looks suspiciously like Clive's dead wife Molly. Eventually she gives up all pretence of being a separate character and speaks both parts, mother and mistress, in the same voice. By this time it hardly matters, as Claud has merged with Clive and Kevin with Claud.

Clive's best memories of his wife Molly have to do with holidays at Cap Ferrat. But Clive can't bring himself to do more than roughly sketch in the backgrounds. He returns again and again to the same verandah, a stage set, backed by a cheap and lurid cyclorama whose painted image changes perfunctorily from scene to scene.

The shape of the story is a mess as well. Old Clive never gets further than setting up a bored, tired, febrile triangle. His real nightmares intrude superciliously. The modes of the story are hopelessly mixed. On the one hand,

10–2, 3. The all-purpose verandah with cyclorama. 2. Claud (Dirk Bogarde) and Sonia (Ellen Burstyn) at Cap Ferrat. 3. Claud and Helen (Elaine Stritch) in 'the city'.

what passes in Clive's mind for serious and realistic drawing-room drama: on the other, a surrealistic fantasy set in a future in which football stadiums have been turned into concentration camps. It's an old man's pessimism. As Clive has Helen say,

Between the terrorist bombing and the demolition of all those lovely old buildings, there soon won't be much left.

It's *Muriel*'s Boulogne in reverse.

Clive knows the image is cant:
Oh, hell! These places are almost becoming de rigueur as fear symbols. Jolly well bloody old de rigueur, eh?

Clive can't get the piece moving. There isn't any action. He's aware of this failing, too. Claud, as Clive writes him, priggishly doesn't approve of violence. 'It reeks of spontaneity.'

Kevin kills one of the incipient wolfmen. 'He said he was dying. He begged me to finish him off.' Death is everything in *Providence*. Claud prosecutes Kevin. Kevin goes free, and immediately takes up with Sonia. Claud is snidely bored by the affair:

I don't actually *smell* the sex.... Hasn't there *been* any?!

Claud takes up with Helen. Dull. A thousand bourgeois British drawing-room dramas. Everyone speaks in well-knit paragraphs. Everyone knows much too much. It's all too, too predictable. It's No Exit. Everyone reviles everyone else and their pleasures consist of finding new ways in which to express the revulsion, the contempt in which they hold their own lives, the errors of the past. Helen asks Claud:

So – how do you and Sonia live?
CLAUD: In a state of unacknowledged mutual exhaustion. We have everything we need. But have we ever had anything we wanted? Successful, civilised, tolerant, intelligent. And somewhere behind it all we scream. We scream. Soundlessly.

It's as if Clive had invented the splenetic, icy Claud simply to serve as a conduit for his failed dialogue, à wastebasket.

But at the same time as Clive is spinning a frayed yarn which does him no credit, his providential master David Mercer is playing tricks, too. As Clive sinks deeper and deeper into the night and the wine and the pain the scenes become less fictional, more dreamlike.

Clive's Claud (David's Clive's Claud) spends more of his time reviling his father. He dictates long letters:

And furthermore, Father. Since there is no point in telephoning you and even less in visiting you ... we would surely do no more than expose ourselves to those now

10–4, 5. The football stadium.... 'de rigueur' as fear symbols

familiar and mutual recriminations ... damn it all, Father, you are a rich man. So if you must do your dying with such ostentatious lack of dignity ... why not do it in a suitable nursing home or some such place where they will at least stand back in amazed and well-paid tolerance. Whilst you drink, shout and protest your way through death's dark door – (*pause*)

The silence when you get to the other side will be our only reassurance that you have actually gone!

Helen – a weak attempt at a character to begin with – falls into playing Molly, the suicide wife and mother. Eventually Clive and Claud, father and son, author and character, are 'mano a mano', slashing at each other with musty family arguments. Clive often loses control. At one point he has the incongruous footballer attack Claud. Claud goes sprawling across the phoney verandah in balletic mock pain. Clive, remorseful, does the scene again.

The one weakness in *Providence* – and it may be fatal for some viewers – is that the story-outside-the-story is nearly as fatuous as the story within the story. Having had Clive's introduction to them, how can we actually care about Clive and Claud and Molly, Sonia and Kevin? One of Clive's periodic apologias seems almost to reach in the other direction, towards Mercer and Resnais.

10–6. Claud on the verandah after being socked by the footballer.

Of course it's been said about my work that the search for style has often resulted in a want of feeling. *(pause)*....However, I'd put it another way. I'd say that style *is* feeling. In its most elegant and economic expression.

Yes, but.... Mercer clearly seems to have felt it was necessary to give his characters the same quality of plot to play out that they would have given themselves. The point of *Providence* is fiction. Cinephiles who know Alain Resnais's obsessions will quickly ascribe the material of *Providence* to him. But Mercer, whose work is not so well known outside England, has been developing in pretty much the same direction.

All the major elements o. the film are Mercer's – at least to begin with (and on the evidence of the screenplay). Claud prosecutes Kevin for shooting an old man. Kevin says he was doing him a favour. The old man was turning into a werewolf. Later, Kevin turns into a werewolf and Claud returns the favour. People have had this hairy propensity in Mercer's work ever since *A Suitable Case For Treatment* (1962), the play which served as a basis for Karel Reisz's film *Morgan* (1965).

During the late sixties, Mercer devoted several stage and television pieces to the type of marital infighting which characterizes Claud and Sonia's marriage, and which provides an elusive secondary interest throughout much of *Providence*. As for the fall into fiction, out of controlled reality, Mercer had a practice run with this in *Duck Song* (1974), a play in which the naturalistic conventions of theatre disintegrate.

In the seventies, filmgoers probably know Mercer best as the author of the screenplay for Ken Loach's *Family Life* (*Wednesday's Child*) (1972) based on his 1967 television play, *In Two Minds*. The differences between the intensely verisimilitudinous Loach film and Resnais's distillation of fiction are striking, of course, but the same impetus gives rise to both. Mercer, who used to be known in the early sixties as a 'political' playwright, has moved increasingly towards a focused concern for individuality: it comes out as schizophrenia in *Family Life*, as novelist's nightmare in *Providence*; both films are obsessed with the damage families do to people. For Clive Langham, fiction is family: what he does, as author, to Claud is fully balanced by what Claud, in Clive's imagination, does to Clive. If Mercer were asked, he might describe this as 'post-political consciousness'. In a trilogy of television plays written in 1969 and 1970, Mercer developed the semi-autobiographical character of 'Robert Kelvin' (who is alluded to in *Providence*) a successful Marxist writer who can't reconcile his function in the capitalist world to his ideals.

This is the basic emotional set of the film: a quasi-paranoid, irreconcilable dichotomy between one's image of oneself and one's image of the self as perceived by others. Clive has Claud sneer at him:

10–7, 8. The film begins with the trial metaphor, one of the facets of which is the continuing struggle between Claud, in control as the prosecutor, and Sonia, an observer on the sidelines. Since Claud stands in for Clive on occasion, the relationship takes on double meaning. As Clive has Sonia explain it later on, 'And so I passed from childhood, more or less; to – er, wifehood? – without the tiresome intervention of a developing personality in between! ... I'm not a person; I'm a fucking construction.'

My father was a great revolutionary, in his time.
(*pause*)
Inside his head.
(*pause*)

Then Claud defines 'post-political man':

What is a bourgeois, Wooders? What if not a person who simply lacks faith in the capacity of human nature for radical transformation?

The comic emblem for Clive's bifurcated view of his children's image of him, and its results in their relationship, is summarized for Resnais by a Groucho Marx story,

about a man who, stuck on the highway at night, wants to ask for help at a nearby residence. Before knocking on the door, he imagines that the people will receive him badly and even throw him out. He rings the doorbell and, as they open, he screams: 'Bastards! won't you help a man who is stuck on the road in the middle of the night!?[3]

What really holds our interest in *Providence* is not the drama, but the play. Clive's nightmare is an actor's dream. Resnais had first experimented with the unique dialectic between star and character in *Stavisky*... Now he lets his actors out at full reign, and audiences react not to character, as they had to in the earlier Resnais films, so much as to actor playing character: less verisimilitude, more craft. There's a sense of thespian sport here.

As Claud, Dirk Bogarde, Resnais's quondam Marquis de Sade, plays with virtuosic, broad panache. He is slimily thin, outrageously effete, thrillingly nasty. He displays an entire category of impetuously fulsome moves and looks. David Warner's Kevin is as dumb and mushy as Bogarde's Claud is sinewy and sharp. Warner, his massive, craggy, pock-marked face looming like a parody of Mount Rushmore, has never hulked better. The two of them are obviously enjoying their music-hall melodrama immensely. John Gielgud, although his Clive is not as stylized and distorted as his Clive's sons, similarly milks a luscious role adeptly.

If Resnais had stopped with these three, however, the result would have added up to little more than high camp. The key to the elaborate role/actor structure lies with the women of the piece. Resnais has purposefully cast two quintessentially American actresses amongst this trio of classic English types. Ellen Burstyn and Elaine Stritch are utterly, thoroughly, magnificently wrong for the roles in which Clive would use them. If one had been able to take Mercer's mock stage dialogue seriously in the mouths of Bogarde, Warner, and Gielgud because at least they're English, any remaining shred of credulity evaporates once Elaine Stritch opens her wonderfully American mouth. The fey British stage speech coagulates in it, sours before it issues forth. Burstyn

10–9, 10. Playacting with style, and playing around with it. Resnais promoted Claud's apartment in the script to a fairly large house in the film as shot. An elaborate set that is absurdly marmoreal and effusive, as are the characters Clive halfheartedly invents. 9. Claud, Kevin, and Sonia in longshot. 10. Sonia posing.

10–11. Claud barely balanced among fey furnishings

10–12. Sonia and Helen, wife and mistress, discuss things while Claud smokes.

10–13, 14. The affair Clive invents for Sonia and Kevin is badly structured. At times, cold and purposeless (like Kevin), it sometimes seems about to break into passion.

might be just believable as a mid-Atlantic accented wife of Bogarde. Stritch, the American mistress/English wife, clearly is not.

Just in case the point might be missed, Tania Lopert is given a show-stopping turn a little later in the film as Claud's secretary. She has listened impassively and mutely through two of his vicious harangues against his dying father. Finally, she has had enough. (Clive has decided to bring her over to his side.) She rips into a short speech, her first, in pure New York defending Clive ending with Clive's clincher:

He's had me more than once! Why shouldn't I be fucked by a genius!

Shades of Judy Holliday. Blackout. Who knows what humour lurks in the imaginations of flatulent, delirious 78-year-old writers? Clive loves the joke. So too, do Mercer and Resnais. It's an ethereal one, but *Providence* is Resnais's first wholehearted comedy.

Interestingly, the script of the film reads more funnily than the finished film sounds. More precisely, there is a depth to the film that isn't so obvious in the script. From the script, one can envisage a film shot with a looser, faster pace, with actors who don't quite have the resonance of the cast Resnais has assembled. You don't hire Gielgud, Bogarde, Stritch, and Burstyn and expect a lightness of tone to characterize the proceedings. They carry with them too many memories.

The irony of the interplay of the fictions Clive invents goes only so far. Three-quarters of the way through *Providence* Resnais and Mercer bring us back to ground. Clive has got ungently through the good night. It is noon. He is sitting in a lawn chair in the sun outside. It is the real outside. Birds sing, crickets chirp, cicadas buzz. Life. 'Where the bee sucks, there suck I.' Reality. We are free of the by now suffocating cycloramas, the self-parodic, half-mad Miklòs Ròsza score, the precious mauve and taupe interiors, the deadening soundtrack, the claustrophobic stagey sets, even the cant dialogue. The effect is exhilarating.

In the long sequence that follows (Act III of Mercer's playlike script), Clive no longer maintains sure fictional control; it has been relinquished to Mercer and Resnais. From all we can see, Claud and Sonia are quite contentedly married (not as Clive would have had it, bitchy characters out of marital melodrama). The 'real' Claud makes a striking contrast with the fiction his father fantasized: stiff, yes, but also subdued, cautious, thoughtful, almost obsequious. It's entirely clear that he finds his father as difficult as his father has dreamt and written that he finds him. But he keeps these feelings quite under control. He is not yet free of his father as Clive thinks he is. He hardly has the cold, satanic wit his father/author ascribed to him last night.

It's Clive's birthday, and his children have brought him presents: a giant

10–15. The patriarch and author awaits his creations....

10–16. ... Who arrive with presents and surprising good will.

penknife, once said to have been owned by Ernest Hemingway ('of course, you know, he wasn't so much of a damned innovator as they all make out,' Clive feels compelled to note). There is also a Victorian telescope ('Now that *is* functional. Specially as I'm half sodding blind these days.'). And a new novel – *The Scales of Time* – by one 'Robert Kelvin'. ('What's this what's this? (*pause*) Not old bumface's latest drivel? Ah Claud, dear boy. Always so maladroit when it comes to presents.') Clive shows proper contempt for the book. What no one tells us is that 'Robert Kelvin' is a refugee from Mercer's semi-autobiographical *On The Eve of Publication* and that Kelvin's picture on the back of the book is David Mercer's. We are not out of the fictional woods yet. (The joke, by the way, seems to have been Resnais's. Mercer's script has it as a book of poems, *The Allegro Sonata*.)

There is still some lugubrious Ròsza to go round. (It's the first time Resnais has used an old Hollywood composer.) And, on second thought, isn't it a bit much for Claud and Kevin (who, we discover, is Clive's 'favourite bastard') to spend all that time in the background marvelling over a baby raccoon? Yes, the last sequence of *Providence* is rather egregious. It's still after all the same Clive Langham (only less so than last night). And once this business of fictionalizing gets started, it's infectious. Resnais's *mise en scène* makes

10–17. The Chateau Américain, imagined in the French countryside by an American architect.

it much clearer than Mercer's script that the mood of the first part of the film has insidiously lapped over into the second part. The trick is that the outdoor birthday party sequence is not by any means so awfully fictive as the first three-quarters of the film. By comparison, it appears starkly verisimilitudinous – and we accept it as such – at least for a while. Also, there is a truth in the fiction. Had Clive had his wits about him last night no doubt he would have been producing better work. If he had, we would have taken it straight.

This last sequence of *Providence* is masterfully ambiguous. Like a perfectly balanced multi-stable figure illusion it shifts back and forth between parody and moral seriousness, and we can't control the oscillations. Is that 360 crane shot just before the end which takes us up from the groaning picnic table in mid-afternoon, carries us around Clive's domain, and sets us down again as evening draws nigh – is that shot as moving as it seems, or is it grandiose? Clive sends his children away, possibly for the last time, with terse magniloquence:

One last thing after this strange and marvellous afternoon.
(*pause*)
Sonia, Claud. Kevin.
(*pause*)
Just leave.
(*pause*)
Now, please.
(*pause*)
With neither kiss nor touch.
(*pause*)
With my blessing –

He stands watching them go. Then after a long pause, in the dusk, as his servants urge him to accompany them into the house:

I think there's time for just one more.

Gielgud brings this off. And he doesn't. It's a moving sentiment. And it's a stylized bit of posing.

Alone at the end, waiting to die, having sent his loving children away, John Gielgud as Clive almost brings it off. As the dusk settles its protective cloak, caressing the brooding old house of Clive Langham's fictions ... he hiccups, and keels over dead. (*No, no, that won't do. Let's try again.*)

... I think there's time for just one more.

Alone at the end with his beloved bottle of Chablis, John Gielgud as Clive settles the dusk over its protective cloak, and the old mansion, bereft of years, croaks. . . .

(*Clearing of the throat.*)

... just one more. Solitary, finally, Gielgud as Clive settles into his chair as the dusk falls and the old house broods. He reaches for the white wine. 'I think,' he says, contented and resigned, 'there is time for just one more. The facts are not in dispute.' He gets up and walks ever so slowly into the house as we pull away, the heavy music starts up again, and the credits roll.

Providence is funnier than you think it is. It's funnier than I thought it was.

Trials

I spoke with Resnais a few days after *Providence* was released in New York. It had received mixed reviews. A couple of major critics had disliked it strongly – and had also grossly misinterpreted it. Resnais had enjoyed making the film, despite the trial of working in English. ('In a sense it was agreeable enough,' he joked, 'because I had the impression of being at the cinema. I was looking for the subtitles in the bottom of the viewfinder of my camera.'[4]) But having just finished editing it, he was tired. He cut from the script only 45 lines of dialogue and 'maybe a dozen images', which is little enough, but 'there comes a time when all you want to do is get a complete print of the film. Nothing else matters'. He had also viewed up till that time eleven prints of the film from end to end to check the colour. He had completely lost his point of view on *Providence*, but one sensed he was more than a little tired of the difficult business of releasing a film, waiting for the critics' judgements, waiting for the box office receipts, to find out if it was going to take six years, or a week, to raise the money for the next project. The proofs of the newspaper advertisements had just come in: a tall list of glowing quotations, carefully culled. Resnais suggested that it would be nice to sneak in just one negative remark – 'an unmitigated disaster!' – in the middle of that praise. It was only partly a joke.

Although Resnais at first benefited from his reputation among critics for being a cinematic intellectual, he has certainly been hurt more than helped by that image over the years. There were high hopes that this first film in English, with stars, would mark a consolidation of the commercial reputation that had begun with *Stavisky...*. *Providence* was being talked about as 'Resnais's most accessible film.' He had a resigned attitude about that image for the film: 'I've often read, after every one of my films, just about: "This time Resnais is clearer!"' In fact, *Providence* seems to me to be, if not Resnais's most 'inaccessible' film, certainly his most subtle. And that has been the problem over the years.

Yet although the daily critics didn't care much for the precision and subtlety of *Providence*, and precious few thought it was funny (as Resnais

10–18. Claud about to ride through Providence.... or is it Arkham?

certainly did), the film is gradually finding its proper audience. As a puzzle, it puts *Marienbad* to shame.

Richard Corliss, writing in *New Times*, was the first to seize on this aspect of the film.[5] Playing the 'lit-crit game, if only for old times' sake', Corliss first notes the literary meaning of the names: Claud: 'lame', Sonia: 'wisdom', Kevin (the love child): 'comely birth', Helen (of Troy) and Molly (Bloom) being the names of literature's two most notoriously unfaithful wives. He then summons up the dictionary definitions of 'providence', which include, 'care or preparation in advance', 'economy', and 'the control exercised by a deity', as well as, of course, the city in Rhode Island. Here's Corliss's coup. 'This, believe it or not,' he announces, 'is the key to the movie.' Providence, R. I. was the lifelong home of H. P. Lovecraft, and Corliss explains the parallels between the fantasy writer of the twenties and thirties and this French intellectual student of pulp fiction in the sixties and seventies.

If this seems a bit of criticism in extremis, then how else to explain why Resnais felt it necessary to come to the U.S. for a week of shooting in and around Providence? The city makes a few brief appearances as part of the fictional landscape Clive constructs for his browbeaten characters. Clive's house itself, however, was in France. ('But not really,' Resnais explains, 'because it was built by Americans with an American architect and they brought not only their own furniture, but their own trees, their own flowers!'[6]) Little things sometimes take on tremendous importance in the imagination. Jacob Münch, the Swiss critic, has gone even further.[7] His own theory of the genesis of *Providence* has to do with an elaborate sociogram of Resnais's personal acquaintances. He begins by noting – as a number of other critics have – that Resnais's father-in-law was dying at the time. He then traces back the peculiar structure of *Providence* along two lines: The first involves Elaine Stritch, whose most prominent stage role was in Stephen Sondheim's *Company*. Noting that Sondheim and Resnais had spent time together working on *Stavisky...* he then goes into an elaborate exegesis of the one film Sondheim has written (with Anthony Perkins), *The Last of Sheila* (Herbert Ross directed in 1973). Now, *The Last of Sheila* is an unbelievably intricate set of puns, anagrams, wordplay, and similar crossword puzzle tricks (it was Sondheim who introduced the British-style crossword puzzle to the U.S. in the late sixties in the pages of *New York* magazine, which is prominently displayed in Clive's imagined living room for Claud and Sonia). After a long list of points of comparison between the two films, which at times certainly strains the limits of credulity, Münch follows his second structural line: David Mercer and David Warner both worked together for the first time in *Morgan*, which was directed by Karel Reisz whom, it is known, Resnais admires greatly. (When I asked him once if there were any books or theories he thought were particularly influential in forming his career, he suggested several standards, but emphasized Reisz's classic practical text, *The Technique of Film Editing*. 'I am sure that Karel Reisz was my real teacher,' he said. 'I took a lot of things from his book. I am not ashamed to say that.')

Münch's conclusion is that *Providence* was for Resnais a way of paying homage to artists he admires (emphasized by the interior homage to David Mercer) and, in addition, a summary of his own work, combining the sense of impending disaster of *Hiroshima*, the cerebral fictional puzzle of *Marienbad*, the architectural symbolism of *Muriel*, and the structural scheme of *Je t'aime* (whereas *Je t'aime* gives us a series of slices through time in the life of one man, *Providence* provides multiple images of several people seen through one creative mind), together with the mordant, pervasive contemplation on death that is *Stavisky*.... Only one of Resnais's films is missing from this catalogue: *La Guerre est finie*. But that was a film about political man, and *Providence* is 'post-political'.

Whether or not one wants to trust this kind of criticism which is clearly more creative synthesis than analytical reportage, two things are clear:

First, much more outrageous critical fantasies are perpetrated daily – hourly – on the literary corpses of writers dead and gone in literature departments and scholarly magazines everywhere. Film has reached the point where it too is now susceptible. We will probably have to bear with this critical over-kill. Clive Langham is aware of it ('He wasn't so much of a damned innovator as they all make out'). And Alain Resnais is also aware of it.

Second, and more germane for our purposes, Alain Resnais – for better or worse – is a prime candidate for this sort of critical imagination. *He* will probably have to bear with it.

There is one scene in *Providence* that stands out emblematically in the memory. Clive has begun the film with a character he can't, ultimately, use – a Dr. Mark Eddington, who seems to have been an old family friend. Clive's first interjection concerns him:

Now who's this bugger?
(*pause*)
Ah yes. The jolly old bloody old Doctor character.

In a moment, he finds out why Eddington's there. An autopsy is performed. A real one. Eddington slits the body of the old man neatly from crotch to head. . . .

So that's it!
(*pause*)
I wish you'd get out of my mind.
(*pause*)
Well I'm going to fight you – see?

It's not just a dramatic correlative for Clive's fear of death. He really has none, not in the sense that most of us understand it. It's more a metaphor for the corpse of his art. We murder to dissect.

Now who's this bugger?
(*pause*)
Ah yes. The jolly old bloody old Director character.

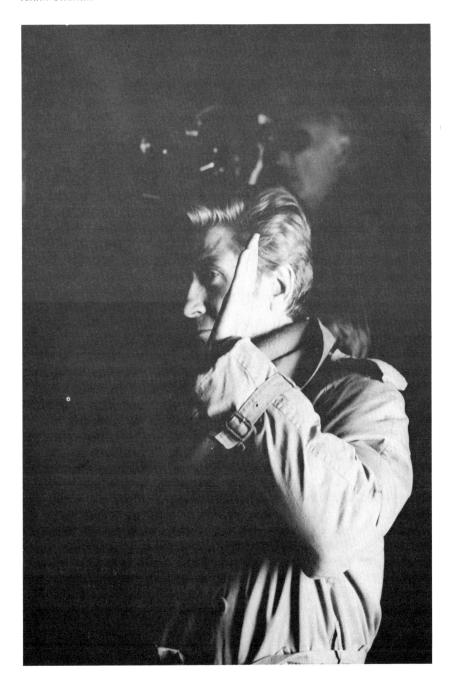

Envoi: Intellection

Ultimately, Alain Resnais's corpus of elegantly conceived and meticulously executed films has the value that it does because it gives us such a vivid, honest, feeling portrait of the artist as intellectual, in the best and truest sense of that word. In French, there is a verb, 'préciser', to make precise. It would be emblazoned on Resnais's shield, if he had one – emblazoned, not inscribed, for he approaches that task with paradoxical gusto. We know measurably more about how our minds work in this world thanks to Resnais's films. He shows us how we put things together, how we take them apart, how we deal with experience and confront death, the end of it. He hasn't yet found a way to make this knowledge popular, and he probably never will, though he works in an artform which has hitherto been identified by its broad appeal, for his talent is markedly introspective. It's his own body the jolly old bloody Director character cuts up.

In twenty years, we have missed a lot of Resnais, we have caught only the public evidence; much remains hidden. When I had the chance to speak with Resnais shortly before I began work on this book I asked him whether he was disappointed by the relatively small number of films he has made. Let him have the last word:

Yes, I am very disappointed. I don't know what it is, whether it's the traffic, or because I spend too much time *trying* to answer mail, or because it's that if you live in a big city, nobody has enough time. I have the feeling that if there was no problem with money I could very easily spend my life without making any films. Maybe I am wrong. Maybe I would miss it. I hate the preparation work. I hate the writing period. But I enjoy the shooting very much. But every day is too short for me. I never manage to do what I want in one day, so sometimes I have the feeling that movie-making is taking too much of my time.

I only think that if I want to read, or listen to all the music I do before I die ... my time is full! eh? If you consider that Josef Haydn has written one hundred symphonies and about thirty quartets and about fifty concertos for different instruments, and I just one month ago discovered Josef Haydn, you see that just listening to two symphonies a day my year will be full till December!

I had a friend once who looked at his library and discovered that even if he completely stopped filmmaking (he was a filmmaker too) and just decided to read the books he had in his library, it would take him until he was 100 years old. He was a little bit panicked.

But he was courageous. He went out of his house. He went to the bookstore. And he bought ten books.

Notes

Chapter 1
1. 'Werewolf, Mon Amour', *New Yorker*, 31 January 1977.
2. 'The Birth of a New Avant Garde: La Caméra-Stylo', in *The New Wave*, ed. Peter Graham. Trans. from *Ecran Français* 144, 30 March 1948.
3. Interview with the author, October 1974.
4. Interview with the author, October 1974.
5. Win Sharples, Jr., 'Alain Resnais', interview, *Filmmakers Newsletter* 8:2 (December 1974).
6. Dan Yakir. 'In the Twilight Zone: 1000 Eyes Talks to Alain Resnais', *1000 Eyes*, March 1977.
7. Penelope Mortimer, 'Resnais Doesn't Look Hungry Anymore', *The Soho Weekly News*, 10 October 1974.
8. *Keywords: A Vocabulary of Culture and Society*, p. 131.
9. 'Salon de 1859', in *Curiosités Esthétiques, Oeuvres Complètes*.

Chapter 2
1. Georges Hilleret, quoted in Gaston Bounoure, *Alain Resnais*, p. 8.
2. Quoted in Bounoure, p. 11.
3. 'Une Expérience', *Ciné-Club* 3 (December 1948).
4. *Cahiers du Cinéma* 92.
5. Quoted in Bounoure, p. 53.
6. *L'Avant-Scène du Cinéma* 1 (15 February 1961).
7. Quoted in Roy Armes, *The Cinema of Alain Resnais*, p. 61.
8. Interview with the author, October 1974.
9. Interview with the author, October 1974.
10. Interview with the author, October 1974.
11. Interview with the author, October 1974.

Chapter 3
1. Quoted in Armes, p. 66.
2. All citations from the script are from Richard Seaver's translation, published by Grove Press.

Chapter 4
1. Quoted in Armes, p. 105.
2. Quoted in Armes, p. 75.
3. Introduction to *Last Year at Marienbad.*
4. All citations from the script are from Richard Howard's translation, published by Grove Press.
5. *A Biographical Dictionary of Cinema.*
6. Introduction to *Last Year at Marienbad.*
7. Introduction to *Last Year at Marienbad.*
8. Quoted in Armes, p. 92.
9. Quoted in Bounoure, p. 68.

Chapter 5
1. Quoted in Bounoure, p. 56.
2. Interview with the author, October 1974.
3. Quoted in Armes, p. 128.
4. Interview with the author, October 1974.
5. Quoted in Armes, p. 129.

Chapter 6
1. Interview with the author, October 1974.
2. See *A Biographical Dictionary of Cinema.*
3. All citations from the script are from Richard Seaver's translation, published by Grove Press.
4. Interview with Pierre Uytterhoeven, *Image et Son* 148 (February 1962), quoted in Armes, p. 131.
5. p. 117.
6. Interview with the author, October 1974.

Chapter 7
1. 'Resnais, est-il un moule à gaufres?', *l'Avant-Scène* 91 (April 1969).
2. All citations from the script are translated from *l'Avant-Scène* edition.
3. 'Resnais, est-il un moule à gaufres?'
4. Interview by Philippe Labro, in *l'Avant-Scène* 91 (April 1969).
5. Interview with the author, October 1974.

Chapter 8
1. Interview with the author, October 1974.
2. 'Resnais Doesn't Look Hungry Anymore', *The Soho Weekly News*, 10 October 1974.
3. Interview with the author, October 1974.
4. Interview with the author, May 1977.
5. All citations from the script and 'Statement of Intentions' are from Seaver's revised manuscript, dated April 1970.

6. Interview with the author, May 1977.
7. All citations from the script are from Lee's final manuscript version, undated.

Chapter 9
1. Interview with the author, October 1974.
2. Interview with the author, May 1977.
3. Richard Seaver, Interview with Alain Resnais, in *Stavisky...*, Viking edition, p. 156.
4. Seaver, p. 162.
5. Interview with the author, October 1974.
6. All citations from the script are from Richard Seaver's edition for the Viking Press, trans. Sabine Destrée.
7. Seaver, p. 156.
8. Seaver, p. 161.
9. Interview with the author, October 1974.
10. Seaver, p. 155.

Chapter 10
1. Dan Yakir.
2. All citations from the script are from a copy of David Mercer's manuscript, 'third draft with additional pages'.
3. Yakir.
4. Interview with the author, January 1977.
5. 'Lit Crit', *New Times*, 4 March 1977.
6. Interview with the author, January 1977.
7. 'Les Sosies de Resnais', *Cinéma Paradigme* (Génève) 5 (26 April 1977).

Filmography

Alain Resnais
Born: Vannes, Brittany, 3 June 1922

Many filmographies of Resnais include ephemera and unfinished projects. The list that follows relies on earlier work – especially the data that have been collected by *l'Avant-Scène* in their various issues devoted to Resnais – and has been revised and edited by Resnais to provide a true picture of his career as he sees it.

Short films:

Fantômas (1935)   Based on the novels by Pierre Souvestre and Marcel Allain. 8 mm (lost). Unfinished.

L'Aventure de Guy (1934)   Script: Gaston Modot. Photography and Editing: Resnais. 8 mm.

Schéma d'une identification (1946)   16 mm silent. With: Gérard Philipe, François Chaumette (lost).

Series about painters (1947): *Visite à Lucien Coutaud, Visite à Félix Labisse, Visite à Hans Hartung, Visite à César Doméla, Portrait de Henri Goetz.*

La Bague (1947)   16 mm, mime. With: Marcel Marceau.

L'Alcoöl tue (1947)   Script: Rémo Forlani, Roland Dubillard. Direction: 'Alzin Rezarail' (Alain Resnais). With: Roland Dubillard, Rémo Forlani, Robert Mendigal (*workmen*), Claude Charpentier (*Priest*), Christiane Renty, Colette Renty (*women*), Paul Renty (*Foreman*). Filmed on location in a quarry near Meaux. 16 mm. Production: Christiane Renty, Paul Renty (Les Films de la Roue).

Le Lait Nestlè (1947)   Two commercials, same titles and credits. Script: Rémo Forlani, Fernand Marzelle, Resnais. Direction: Forlani, Marzelle, Resnais. Photography and Editing: Resnais. Production: l'Agence ABC. Shot in maternity hospital at Montmorency. Running times: 1 min. each.

Van Gogh (1948)   Script: Robert Hessens, Gaston Diehl. Photography: Henri Ferrand. Sound: Studios Saint-Maurice. Music: Jacques Besse. Narrator: Claude Dauphin. Production: Claude Hauser, for Pierre Braunberger. Remake in 35 mm of original 16 mm version (1947). Premiere: Paris, May 1948. Running time: 20 min.

Malfray (1948)   Direction: Resnais, Robert Hessens. Script: Gaston Diehl, Robert Hessens. Music: Pierre Barbaud. 16 mm.

Gauguin (1950)   Script: Gaston Diehl. Photography: Henri Ferrand. Music: Darius Milhaud. Narrator: Jean Servais. Production: Pierre Braunberger (Pantheon). Premiere: Paris, June 1951. Running time: 11 min.

Guernica (1950)   Script: Robert Hessens. Photography: Henri Ferrand. Music: Guy Bernard. Sound: Pierre-Louis Calvet. Text: Paul Eluard. Narrators: Maria Casarès, Jacques Pruvost. Production: Claude Hauser, for Pierre Braunberger (Pantheon). Premiere: Paris, June 1950. Running time: 12 min.

Les Statues meurent aussi (1950–3)   Script: Chris Marker. Direction: Resnais, Chris Marker. Photography: Ghislain Cloquet. Music: Guy Bernard. Sound: Studio Marignan. Narrator: Jean Negroni. Production: Présence Africaine/Tadié-Cinéma. Only showing: Cannes Festival, May 1953. Running time: 30 min.

Nuit et Brouillard (1955)   Commentary: Jean Cayrol. Photography: Ghislain Cloquet, Sacha Vierny (part Eastmancolor). Music: Hanns Eisler. Historical advisers: Henri Michel, Olga Wormser. Assistant director: André Heinrich. Editing: Henri Colpi, Jasmine Chasney. Narrator: Michel Bouquet. Production: Argos/Como/ Cocinor. Premiere: Cannes Festival, 8 May 1956. Running time: 31 min.

Toute la mémoire du monde (1956)   Script: Rémo Forlani. Photography: Ghislain Cloquet. Editing: Resnais. Music: Maurice Jarre (director: Georges Delerue). Sound: Studio Marignan. Narrator: Jacques Dumesnil. Production: Pierre Braunberger (Les Films de la Pléiade). 'With the collaboration of: Gérard Willemetz, Pierre Goupil, Anne Sarraute, Roger Fleytoux, Claude Joudioux, Jean Cayrol, André Goefers, Jean-Claude Lauthe, Chris and Magic Marker, Phil Davis, Robert Rendigal, Giuletta Caput, Claudine Merlin, Dominique Raoul Duval, Chester Gould, Denise York, Benigno Caceres, Agnès Varda, Monique le Porrier, Paulette Borker, André Heinrich, Mme. Searle, Marie-Claire Pasquier, François-Régis Bastide, Joseph Rovan.' Shot at the Bibliothèque Nationale, Paris.

Le Mystère de l'atelier 15 (1957)   Commentary: Chris Marker. Direction: Resnais, André Heinrich. Photography: Ghislain Cloquet, Sacha Vierny. Editing: Anne Sarraute. Music: Pierre Barbaud (direction: Georges Delerue). Sound: Studio Marignan. Narrator: Jean-Pierre Grenier. Technical supervisors: André Vallaud, Georges Smagghe. Production: Jacqueline Jacoupy (Les Films Jacqueline Jacoupy). 'With the collaboration of: Chris Marker, Yves Peneau, Jean Brugot, Fernand Marzelle, Claude Joudioux, André Schlotter, Fearless Fosdick, Elisabeth Seibel.' Running time: 18 min. (This is the only surviving episode of *L'Organization du Travail* which was to have been a series of 40 16-mm documentaries written by Forlani and directed by Resnais.)

Le Chant du Styrène (1958)   Text: Raymond Queneau. Photography: Sacha Vierny (Dyaliscope, Eastmancolor). Music: Pierre Barbaud (direction: Georges Delerue). Editing: Resnais. Narrator: Pierre Dux. Production: Pierre Braunberger (La Société Pechiney). Running time: 19 min. Venice Festival, 1958.

Early Feature:

Ouvert pour cause d'inventaire (1946)   16 mm. With: Danièle Delorme, Michel Auclair, Pierre Trabaud (lost).

Feature Films:

Hiroshima mon amour (1959)

Script	Marguerite Duras
Photography	Sacha Vierny (France), Michio Takahashi (Japan)
Sound	Pierre Calvet (France), Yamamoto (Japan)

Editing	Henri Colpi, Jasmine Chasney, Anne Sarraute
Mixing	René Renault
Art direction	Esaka, Mayo, Petri
Costumes	Gérard Collery
Music	Giovanni Fusco, Georges Delerue
Literary Adviser	Gérard Jarlot
Assistant directors	T. Andréfouet, J.-P. Léon, R. Guyonnet, I. Shirai, Itoi, Hara
Production	Sacha Kamenka, Shirakawa Takeo, for Samy Halfon [Argos Films/Como Films (Paris)/Daieï (Tokyo)/Pathé Overseas].

Shot on location in Hiroshima and Nevers, interiors in Tokyo and Studios Paris, September–December 1958.
Premiere: Cannes Festival, 8 May 1959.
Running time: 91 min.
With: Emmanuèle Riva (*She*), Eiji Okada (*He*), Bernard Fresson (*The German*), Stella Dassas (*The Mother*), Pierre Barbaud (*The Father*).

L'Année dernière à Marienbad (1961)

Script	Alain Robbe-Grillet
Photography	Sacha Vierny (Dyaliscope)
Sound	Guy Villette
Editing	Henri Colpi, Jasmine Chasney
Art direction	Jacques Saulnier
Costumes	Bernard Evein, Chanel
Music	Francis Seyrig (Direction: André Girard)
Assistant director	Jean Léon
Production	Léon Sanz, for Raymond Froment (Terra-Film), Pierre Courau (Précitel) [Terra-Film/ Société Nouvelle des Films/Cormoran/Précitel/ Silver Films (Paris)/Cineriz (Rome)]

Shot on location in Munich, at Nymphenburg, Schleissheim, and other chateaux, and at Photosonor Studios, Paris, September–November 1960.
Premiere: Venice Festival, 29 August 1961.
Running time: 94 min.
U.S./G.B. Title: 'Last Year at Marienbad'.
With: Delphine Seyrig (*A*), Giorgio Albertazzi (*X*), Sacha Pitoëff (*M*), Françoise Bertin, Luce Garcia-Ville, Héléna Kornel, Françoise Spira, Karin Toeche-Mittler, Pierre Barbaud, Wilhelm Von Deek, Jean Lanier, Gérard Lorin, Davide Montemuri, Gilles Quéant, Gabriel Werner.

Muriel, ou le temps d'un retour (1963)

Script	Jean Cayrol
Photography	Sacha Vierny (Eastmancolor)
Sound	Antoine Bonfanti
Editing	Kenout Peltier, Eric Pluet
Art direction	Jacques Saulnier
Music	Hans Werner Henze
Singer	Rita Streich
Song	'Déja', Paul Colline, Paul Maye
Assistant director	Jean Léon
Production	Philippe Dussart, for Anatole Dauman [Argos Films/Alpha Productions/Eclair/Films de la Pléiade (Paris)/Dear Film (Rome)]

Shot on location in Boulogne-sur-Mer, and at Studios Du Mont, Epinay-sur-Seine, November 1962–January 1963.
Premiere: Paris, 24 July 1963.
Running time: 116 min.
With: Delphine Seyrig (*Hélène Aughain*), Jean-Pierre Kerien (*Alphonse Noyard*), Nita Klein (*Françoise*), Jean-Baptiste Thierrée (*Bernard*), Claude Sainval (*Roland de Smoke*), Jean Champion (*Ernest*), Laurence Badie (*Claudie*), Martine Vatel (*Marie-Do*), Philippe Laudenbach (*Robert*), Jean Dasté (*Man with the Goat*), Robert Bordenave (*The Croupier*), Gaston Joly (*Antoine, the tailor*), Catherine de Seynes (*Angèle, the tailor's wife*), Julien Verdier (*The Stableman*), Gérard Lorin, Françoise Bertin, Wanda Kerien, Jean-Jacques Lagarde.

La Guerre est finie (1966)

Script	Jorge Semprun
Photography	Sacha Vierny
Sound	Antoine Bonfanti
Editing	Eric Pluet
Art direction	Jacques Saulnier
Music	Giovanni Fusco
Narrator	Jorge Semprun
Assistant directors	Jean Léon, Florence Malraux
Production	Alain Quéfféléan, for Catherine Winter, Giselle Rebillon [Sofracima (Paris)/Europa-Film (Stockholm)]

Shot on location in Stockholm and Paris, August–November 1965.
Premiere: Cannes Festival, 9 May 1966.
Running time: 121 min.
G.B. Title: 'The War is Over'.
With: Yves Montand (*Diego Mora*), Ingrid Thulin (*Marianne*), Geneviève Bujold

(*Nadine Sallanches*), Dominique Rozan (*Jude*), Françoise Bertin (*Carmen*), Michel Piccoli (*Customs Inspector*), Paul Crauchet (*Roberto*), Gérard Séty (*Bill*), Jean Bouise (*Ramon*), Anouk Ferjac (*Madame Jude*), Yvette Etiévant (*Yvette*), Jean Dasté (*The Chief*), Annie Fargue (*Agnès*), Gérard Lartigau (*Head of students' revolutionary group*), Jacques Rispal (*Manolo*), Jean-François Rémi (*Juan*), Pierre Leproux (*Maker of forged papers*), Marie Mergey (*Madame Lopez*), Marcel Cuvelier (*Inspector Chardin*), Roland Monod (*Antoine*), Bernard Fresson (*Sarlat*), Laurence Badie (*Bernadette Pluvier*), José-María Flotats (*Miguel*), Catherine de Seynes (*Jeanine*), Claire Duhamel (*Traveller*), Jean Larroquette (*Student*), Martine Vatel (*Student*), R.-J. Chauffard (*Tramp*), Antoine Vitez (*Air France employee*), Jacques Robnard (*Pierrot*), Paillette (*Old Woman*), Jacques Wallet (*Security Policeman*), Pierre Decazes (*Railway worker*), Jean Bolo (*Policeman*) Pierre Barbaud (*A client*).

Loin du Vietnam (1967)

Co-direction	William Klein, Joris Ivens (Agnès Varda), Claud Lelouch, Jean-Luc Godard
Script	Jacques Sternberg, rewritten by the team
Photography	Jean Boffety, and Denys Clerval, Ghislain Cloquet
Sound	Antoine Bonfanti
Editing	Colette Semprun and others
Production	SLON (Chris Marker)

Premiere: Montreal Festival, August 1967.
Running time: Entire film: 115 min. Resnais's section: c. 15 min.
U.S./G.B. Title: 'Far From Vietnam'.
With: Bernard Fresson (*Claude Ridder*) and Karen Blanguernon

Je t'aime, je t'aime (1968)

Script	Jacques Sternberg
Photography	Jean Boffety (Eastmancolor)
Sound	Antoine Bonfanti
Editing	Colette Leloup, Albert Jurgenson
Mixing	Jean Neny
Art direction	Jacques Dugied, Auguste Pace
Music	Krzysztof Penderecki; additional music by Jean-Claude Pelletier
Chorus	I Musici Cantati di Varsova
Assistant directors	Florence Malraux, Jean Lefevre
Production	Philippe Dussart, for Mag Bodard (Parc-Film/Fox-Europa)

Shot on location in Brussels, Provence, Paris, northern beaches, 4 September 1967–10 November 1967.
Premiere: Paris, 26 April 1968.
Running time: 91 min.
With: Claude Rich (*Claude Ridder*), Olga Georges-Picot (*Catrine*), Anouk Ferjac (*Wiana Lust*), Georges Jamin (*Dr. Delavoix, clinic surgeon*), Van Doude (*Rouffers, centre chief*), Dominique Rozan (*Dr. Haesserts*), Ray Verhaege (*Goofers, technician*), Yves Kerboul (*Kammers, technician*), Vania Vilers (*Rhuys, technician*), Pierre Barbaud (*Levino, technician*), Alain MacCoy (*Moyens, technician*), Bernard Fresson (*Bernard Hannecart*), Irène Tunc (*Marcelle Hannecart*), Yvette Etievant (*Germaine Coster*), Annie Fargue (*Agnès de Smet, the woman at the bar*), Marie-Blanche Vergne (*Marie-Noire Demoor, the woman on the tram and the stairs*), Carla Marlier (*Nicole Yseux*), Annie Bertin (*Hélène Wiertz, the young mother*), Alain Robbe-Grillet (*Hughes Mechelynck, press attache*), Catherine Robbe-Grillet (*Maryse de Neten, secretary*), Jean Michaud (*publisher*), Allan Adair (*Glasgow, 1st Inspector*), Ian MacGregor (*Glasgow, 2nd Inspector*), Hélène Callot (*Odile Piquet, nurse*), Gérard Lorin (*Guy Puyaubert, dentist*), Jean-Louis Richard (*Friend in the Dining Car*), Jacques Doniol-Valcroze (*Francis Devos, editor*), François Regis-Bastide (*Hubert Brun, party host*), Jean-Claude Romer (*guest*), Francis Lacassin, Bernard Valdeneige, Jean Martin, Georges Walter (*editors*), René Bazart, Billy Fasbender (*employees*), Jean Perre (*Frédéric Poels, editor*), Sylvain Dhomme (*Louis Lambert*), Ben Danou (*Dr. Uyttenhoef*), Pierre Motte (*Edward Monnot*), Michel Blondel, Walter Plinge, Michel Choquet, M. Floquet, Jorge Semprun, Guilene Pean, Alain Tercinet, and others.

Stavisky... (1974)

Script	Jorge Semprun
Photography	Sacha Vierny (Eastmancolor)
Camera	Philippe Brun
Sound	Jean-Pierre Ruh, Bernard Bats
Editing	Albert Jurgenson
Mixing	Jacques Maumont
Art direction	Jacques Saulnier
Costumes	Jacqueline Moreau, Yves-Saint Laurent (Duperey), F. Smalto (Rich)
Music	Stephen Sondheim
Orchestration and supervision	Jonathan Tunick
Automobiles	Musée de l'Anthologie Automobile, Gaillard
Assistant directors	Jean Léon, Florence Malraux, Philippe Lopès
Production	Alain Belmondo, for Alexandre Mnouchkine and Georges Dancigers [Cerito Films/Ariane Films (Paris)/Euro International (Rome)]

Shot in the autumn of 1973 on location in Biarritz, Paris and suburbs.
Premiere: Cannes Festival, May 1974.
Running time: 117 min.
With: Jean-Paul Belmondo (*Serge/Alexandre*), François Périer (*Albert Borelli*), Anny
Duperey (*Arlette*), Michael Lonsdale (*Dr. Mézy*), Robert Bisacco (*Juan Montalvo*),
Claude Rich (*Bonny*), Charles Boyer (*Baron Raoul*), Pierre Vernier (*Pierre Grammont,
lawyer*), Marcel Cuvelier (*Inspector Boussaud*), Van Doude (*Inspector Gardet*), Jacques
Spiesser (*Michel Granville*), Michel Beaune (*journalist*), Maurice Jacquemont
(*Gauthier*), Silvia Badesco (*Erna Wolfgang*), Jacques Eyser (*Véricourt*), Fernand Guiot
(*Van Straaten*), Daniel Lecourtois (*President of the Inquest*), Gérard Depardieu
(*Inventor of the Matriscope*), Nike Arrighi (*Edith Boréal*), Samson Fainsilber,
Raymond-Girard (*Dr. Pierre*), Gigi Ballista (*Gaston Henriet*), Guido Cerniglia
(*Laloy*), Yves Brainville (*M. de la Salle*), Gabriel Cattand (*deputy*), Jean Michaux
(*Houriaux*), Roland Bertin (*cemetery guard*), Niels Arestrup (*Rudolph, Trotsky's
secretary*), Imelde Marani (*provincial woman*), Lucienne Legrand (*Dr. Pierre's nurse*),
Guy Pierauld, Yves Peneau (*Trotsky*), Dominique Rollin (*Sedov*), Catherine Sellers
(*Natalya*), Paul Ville (*Huissier*), François Leterrier (*André Malraux*), Vicky Messica,
Lionel Vitrant, Georges Yacoubian, Jean-Michel Charlier, Jean Davy.

Providence (1977)

Script	David Mercer
Photography	Ricardo Aronovitch (Eastmancolor)
Camera	Philippe Brun
Sound	René Magnol, Jacques Maumont
Editing	Albert Jurgenson, Jean-Pierre Besnard
Mixing	Jacques Maumont
Art direction	Jacques Saulnier
Costumes	Liselle Roos, Catherine Leterrier
Music	Miklòs Ròsza. (National Philharmonic Orchestra directed by the composer)
Assistant directors	Florence Malraux, Reynald Lampert
Production	Philippe Dussart, for Yves Gasser, Klaus Hellwig, and Yves Peyrot [Action Films, Société Française de Production, and FR3 (Paris), and Citel Films (Geneva)]
Associate producers	Lise Fayolle, Jurgen Hellwig

Shot on location in France, Belgium (Louvain, Antwerp, Limoges) and New England
(Providence), and in studios in Paris, April–July 1976.
Premiere: New York, 25 January 1977.
Running time: 110 min.
With: Dirk Bogarde (*Claud Langham*), Ellen Burstyn (*Sonia Langham*), John Gielgud
(*Clive Langham*), David Warner (*Kevin Woodford*), Elaine Stritch (*Helen Wiener* and
Molly Langham), Samson Fainsilber (*the old man*), Cyril Luckham (*Dr. Mark*

Eddington), Tania Lopert (*Miss Lister*), Denis Lawson (*Dave Woodford, the football player*), Kathryn Leigh-Scott (*Miss Boon*), Milo Sperber (*the tailor*), Peter Arne (*Nils, servant*), Anna Wing (*Karen, servant*), Joseph Pittoors (*an old man*).

Bibliography

Scripts:

Van Gogh:
  L'Avant-Scène du Cinéma 61–62 (July–September 1966).

Guernica:
  L'Avant-Scène du Cinéma 38 (June 1964).

Les statues meurent aussi:
  in Chris Marker. *Commentaires*. Paris: Editions du Seuil. 1961.

Nuit et Brouillard:
  L'Avant-Scène du Cinéma 1 (February 1961) (narration only).
  Night and Fog, in *Film: Book II: Films of War and Peace*, ed. Robert Hughes.
  New York; Grove Press. 1962.

Toute la mémoire du monde:
  L'Avant-Scène du Cinéma 52 (October 1965).

Le Mystère de l'atelier quinze:
  L'Avant-Scène du Cinéma 61–62 (July–September 1966).

Le Chant du Styrène:
  L'Avant-Scène du Cinéma 1 (February 1961) (commentary only).

Hiroshima mon amour:
  Marguerite Duras. *Hiroshima mon amour*. Paris: Gallimard. 1960. Translated in
  German in *Spektakulum: Texte Moderner Filme*. Frankfurt: Suhrkamp Verlag.
  1961. English translation by Richard Seaver. New York: Grove Press. 1961.
  London: Calder and Boyars. 1966.
  L.Avant-Scène du Cinéma 61–62 (July–September 1966).

L'Année dernière à Marienbad:
Alain Robbe-Grillet. *L'Année dernière à Marienbad*. Paris: Editions de Minuit.
1961. *Last Year at Marienbad*, English translation by Richard Howard. London:
John Calder. 1961. New York: Grove Press. 1962.

Muriel, ou le temps d'un retour:
Jean Cayrol. *Muriel, ou le temps d'un retour*. Paris: Editions du Seuil. 1964.

La Guerre est finie:
Jorge Semprun. *La Guerre est finie*. Paris: Gallimard. 1966. English translation by
Richard Seaver. New York: Grove Press. 1967.

Je t'aime, je t'aime:
L'Avant-Scène du Cinéma 91 (April 1969).
Jacques Sternberg. *Je t'aime, je t'aime*. Paris: Terrain Vague. 1969.

Stavisky... :
L'Avant-Scène du Cinéma 156 (March 1975).
Jorge Semprun. *Le 'Stavisky' d'Alain Resnais*. Paris: Editions Gallimard. 1974.
Stavisky..., English translation by Sabine Destrée, includes introduction by Richard
Seaver and interview with Resnais by Seaver. New York: A Richard Seaver Book/
The Viking Press. 1975.

Providence:
L'Avant-Scène du Cinéma 195 (1 November 1977).
David Mercer. *Providence*. New York: A Richard Seaver Book/The Viking Press.
1978.

Photographs by Resnais:

Repérages, with an introduction by Jorge Semprun. Paris: Editions du Chêne. 1974.
Resnais's location studies, many for films never realized.

Books about Resnais:

Armes, Roy. *The Cinema of Alain Resnais*. London: A. Zwemmer Ltd., New York:
A. S. Barnes Co. 1968. (*International Film Guide* series.)
Bounoure, Gaston. *Alain Resnais*. Paris: Editions Seghers. 1962. Collection Cinéma
d'aujourd'hui 5. Revised 1974.
Cordier, Stéphane, ed. *Alain Resnais, ou la Création au Cinéma*. Paris. 1961. (*l'Arc* 31.)
Delahaye, Michel and Henri Colpi. *Alain Resnais: Hiroshima Resnais*. Lyon: Serdoc.
1959. (Premier Plan 4, pamph.)
Estève, Michel, ed. *Alain Resnais et Alain Robbe-Grillet: Evolution d'une écriture*. Paris:
Lettres Modernes, Collection Etudes cinématographiques, nos. 100–103.

Pingaud, Bernard. *Alain Resnais*. Lyon: Serdoc. 1961. (Premier Plan 18.)

Ravar, Raymond, ed. *Tu n'as rien vu à Hiroshima*. Brussels: Université Libre de Bruxelles. 1962.

Ward, John. *Alain Resnais, or the Theme of Time*. London: Secker and Warburg, New York: Doubleday. 1968. (Cinema One Series.)

Major Interviews and Profiles:

Archer, Eugene. 'Director of Enigmas', *New York Times Magazine*, 18 March 1962.

Baby, Yvonne. Interview. *Lettres Françaises* 118 (April 1957).

—— Interview. *Le Monde*, 29 August 1961.

—— Interview. *Le Monde*, 11 May 1966.

Benayoun, Robert. Interview. *Positif* 50–2 (March 1963).

Beylie, Claude. 'Alain Resnais, Jorge Semprun et "Stavisky"', *Ecran* 27 (July 1974).

Billard, Pierre. Interview with Resnais and Jean Cayrol. *Cinéma 63* 80 (November 1963). Reprinted in Cayrol: *Muriel*.

Burch, Noel. 'A Conversation With Alain Resnais', *Film Quarterly* 13:3 (Spring 1970).

Delahaye, Michel. Interview. *Cinéma 59* 38 (July 1959).

Egly, Max. Interview. *Image et Son* 128 (February 1960).

Elbhar, R. 'L'Exil est finie (un entretien avec Alain Resnais)', *Séquences* XIX:76 (April 1974).

Gauthier, Guy. Interview. *Image et Son* 196 (July 1966).

Labarthe, André S. and Rivette, Jacques. Interview. *Cahiers du Cinéma* 123 (September 1961). Translated by Raymond Durgnat in *Films and Filming* 8:5 (February 1962): 'Trying to Understand My Own Film', and by Rose Kaplin in *New York Film Bulletin* 3:2 (1962): 'Alain Resnais Speaks at Random'. Reprinted in Andrew Sarris. *Interviews with Film Directors*. Indianapolis: Bobbs-Merrill. 1967. London: Secker and Warburg. 1972.

Labro, Philippe. 'Alain Resnais: Toujours Fidèle à André Breton', (interview), *L'Avant-Scène du Cinéma* 91 (April 1969).

Maben, Adrian. 'Alain Resnais: The War is Over', *Films and Filming* 13:1 (October 1966).

Marcorelles, Louis, Henri Colpi, Richard Roud. 'Alain Resnais and *Hiroshima, Mon Amour*', *Sight and Sound* 29:1 (Winter 1959–60).

Martin, Marcel. Interview. *Cinéma 65* 91–92 (December 1964, January 1965).

Monaco, James. 'Conversations with Resnais: There Isn't Enough Time', *Film Comment* 11:4 (July–August 1975).

Mortimer, Penelope. 'Resnais Doesn't Look Hungry Any More', *The Soho Weekly News*, 10 October 1974.

Pieri, F. and Tassone, A. 'Entretien avec Alain Resnais', *Image et Son* 284 (May 1974). On *Stavisky...* .

Resnais, Alain. Comments. *L'Avant-Scène du Cinéma* 61–62 (July–September 1966).

Rosenbaum, Jonathan. 'Journals: Paris', *Film Comment* 10:2 (March–April 1974). On the shooting of *Stavisky...* and unrealized projects.

Roud, Richard. 'The Left Bank', *Sight and Sound* 32:1 (Winter 1962–63). On Resnais, Marker, and Varda.

——. 'Memories of Resnais', *Sight and Sound* 38:3 (Summer 1969).

——. 'If It's Tuesday, It Must Be Belgium', *Sight and Sound* 45:3 (Summer 1976).

Seaver, Richard. 'Facts Into Fiction', *Film Comment* 11:4 (July–August 1975). Interview. Also printed in Seaver's edition of *Stavisky...* .

Sharples, Win, Jr. 'Alain Resnais: The Freeing of Film Form', *Filmmakers Newsletter* 8:2 (December 1974) (interview).

Truffaut, François. Interview. *Arts*, 20 February 1965.

Uytterhoeven, Pierre. Interview. *Image et Son* 148 (February 1962).

Yakir, Dan. 'In the Twilight Zone' (interview), *1000 Eyes*, March 1977.

Also:

Beatts, Anne. 'Conversation with Stan Lee', *Oui*, March 1977.

Dhomme, Sylvain. 'Jacques Sternberg: Resnais est-il un Moule à Gaufres?' (interview), *L'Avant-Scène du Cinéma* 91 (April 1969).

Roud, Richard. 'Conversation with Marguerite Duras', *Sight and Sound* 29:1 (Winter 1959–60).

Wu, Ying Ying. 'Ellen Burstyn Talks', *Take One* 5:8 (March 1977).

Selected Critical Articles:

Armes, Roy. 'Resnais and Reality', *Films and Filming* 16:8 (May 1970).

——. 'Alain Resnais', in *French Cinema Since 1946*, vol. 2. London: A. Zwemmer Ltd., New York: A. S. Barnes Co. 1966, 1970.

Bazin, André. 'Alain Resnais', in *Qu'est-ce que le cinéma?*, vol. 2. Paris. Editions du Cerf. 1959.

Beylie, Claude. 'L'Année dernière à Chamonix', *L'Avant-Scène du Cinéma* 156 (March 1975).

Colpi, Henri. 'Editing *Hiroshima mon amour*', *Sight and Sound* 29:1 (Winter 1960).

Corliss, Richard. 'Lit Crit', (review of *Providence*), *New Times*, 4 March 1977.

Cowie, Peter. 'Resnais', in *Antonioni – Bergman – Resnais*. London: Tantivy. 1963.

——. 'Alain Resnais', in *International Film Guide 1973*, ed. Peter Cowie. London: Tantivy Press, New York: A. S. Barnes. 1972.

Dawson, Janet. Review of *Hiroshima mon amour*, *Oxford Opinion* IV:9 (6 February 1960).

Discussion of *Hiroshima mon amour*, 96 (July 1959).

Discussion of *Muriel*, 159 (November 1963).

'Film et Roman: Problemes du Récit', 185 (December 1966).

Goldmann, Annie. *'Muriel'* and *'L'Année dernière à Marienbad'*, in *Cinéma et Société Moderne*. Paris: Editions Anthropos. 1971.

Harcourt, Peter. 'Memory is Kept Alive With Dreams', *Film Comment* 9:6 (November–December 1973).

———. 'Alain Resnais: Toward the Certainty of Doubt', *Film Comment* 10:1 (January–February 1974).

Houston, Penelope. *'L'Année dernière à Marienbad'*, *Sight and Sound* 31:1 (Winter 1961–62).

———. Review of *Muriel*, *Sight and Sound* (33:1) (Winter 1963–64).

Jebb, Julian. Review of *Je t'aime, je t'aime*, *Sight and Sound* 40:3 (Summer 1971).

Kael, Pauline. 'Werewolf, Mon Amour' (review of *Providence*), *New Yorker*, 31 January 1977.

Labarthe, Andre S. 'Marienbad Année Zéro', *Cahiers du Cinéma* 123 (September 1961).

Lacassin, Francis. 'Dick Tracy Meets Muriel', *Sight and Sound* 36:2 (Spring 1967).

———. 'Alain Resnais and the Quest for Harry Dickson', *Sight and Sound* 42:4 (Autumn 1973).

Marcorelles, Louis. 'Rebel With a Camera', *Sight and Sound* 29:1 (Winter 1960).

Monaco, James. 'La Recherche des Images Perdus' (review of *Stavisky...*), *Take One* 4:6 (November 1974).

———. 'Alain Resnais's Providence' (review), *Take One* 5:8 (March 1977).

Münch, Jacob. 'Les Sosies de Resnais', *Cinema Paradigme* (Génève) 5 (26 April 1977).

Nowell-Smith, Geoffrey. 'Alain Resnais', *New Left Review* 27 (September–October 1964).

Oxenhandler, Neal. *'Marienbad*. Revisited', *Film Quarterly* 17:1 (Fall 1963).

Pechter, William S. 'On Alain Resnais', *Moviegoer* 1 (Winter 1964).

Prédal, René. 'Un Cinéma Politique: l'Oeuvre de Resnais', *Image et Son* 210 (November 1967).

Rhode, Eric. 'Resnais', in *Tower of Babel*. London: Weidenfeld and Nicolson. 1966.

Robbe-Grillet, Alain. *'L'Année dernière à Marienbad'*, *Sight and Sound* 30:4 (Autumn 1961).

Sadoul, Georges. 'Notes on a New Generation', *Sight and Sound* 28:3–4 (Autumn 1959).

Schreivogel, Paul A. *Night and Fog*. Dayton, Ohio: Pflaum. 1970 (pamph.)

Sontag, Susan, Review of *Muriel*, *Film Quarterly* XVII:2 (Winter 1963–64).

Stanbrook, Alan. 'The Time and Space of Alain Resnais', *Films and Filming* 10:4 (January 1964).

Taylor, John Russell. 'Alain Resnais', in *Cinema Eye, Cinema Ear*. London: Methuen, New York: Hill and Wang. 1964.

Van Wert, William F. *In the Theory and Practice of the Ciné-Roman*. Indiana University dissertation. 1975. New York: Arno Press. 1978.

Index